Advanced Introduction to Planning Theory

Elgar Advanced Introductions are stimulating and thoughtful introductions to major fields in the social sciences and law, expertly written by the world's leading scholars. Designed to be accessible yet rigorous, they offer concise and lucid surveys of the substantive and policy issues associated with discrete subject areas.

The aims of the series are two-fold: to pinpoint essential principles of a particular field, and to offer insights that stimulate critical thinking. By distilling the vast and often technical corpus of information on the subject into a concise and meaningful form, the books serve as accessible introductions for undergraduate and graduate students coming to the subject for the first time. Importantly, they also develop well-informed, nuanced critiques of the field that will challenge and extend the understanding of advanced students, scholars and policy-makers.

For a full list of titles in the series please see the back of the book. Recent titles in the series include:

Advanced Introduction to

Planning Theory

ROBERT A. BEAUREGARD

Professor Emeritus, Columbia University, USA

Elgar Advanced Introductions

Edward Elgar
PUBLISHING

Cheltenham, UK • Northampton, MA, USA

Published by
Edward Elgar Publishing Limited
The Lypiatts
15 Lansdown Road
Cheltenham
Glos GL50 2JA
UK

Edward Elgar Publishing, Inc.
William Pratt House
9 Dewey Court
Northampton
Massachusetts 01060
USA

A catalogue record for this book
is available from the British Library

Library of Congress Control Number: 2019956523

MIX
Paper from
responsible sources
FSC
www.fsc.org   FSC® C013056

ISBN 978 1 78897 888 0 (cased)
ISBN 978 1 78897 890 3 (paperback)
ISBN 978 1 78897 889 7 (eBook)

Typeset by Servis Filmsetting Ltd, Stockport, Cheshire
Printed and bound in Great Britain by TJ International Ltd, Padstow, Cornwall

Theory is what keeps us from being seduced by reality.

Contents

Acknowledgements

I am extremely grateful to Laura Lieto and John West, who provided useful and insightful comments on the manuscript, and to Daphne Spain and Valerie Stahl for more selective but no less helpful readings. At Edward Elgar, I want to thank David Adams (for his editing), Conor Byrne and Stephanie Hartley for their general assistance, and especially Stephen Harries for inviting me to be part of Elgar Advanced Introductions. As always: Debra Bilow for her support and patience.

1   Introduction

Planning seems a commonsense proposition. Young couples save money for the eventual purchase of a home. A concert pianist sets aside time to practice prior to an upcoming engagement. Anticipating a cold and rainy winter, people purchase a new pair of boots and a warmer coat. Each of these activities and the decisions that accompany them involve planning and most people would readily recognize this. In these situations, anticipating the future and acting accordingly appear reasonable.

While the intent of planning in the personal realm is for the most part clear, and how it is done more or less obvious, in organizational and public settings planning becomes more complicated. Often contested, it can be a challenge to manage. For a multinational corporation to expand production in response to an ever-changing global market, it has to undertake elaborate studies, assess alternative economic scenarios, consult with outside investors, and model the impacts on its various divisions before deciding how to finance and where to build new facilities. Matters become even more problematic when democratic governments attempt to influence capital investment, regulate property rights, or borrow funds to subsidize a new sports stadium. Here, planning is likely to be drawn into political controversies. Entangled in ideological debates, questions are raised about the legitimate obligations of government and the relationships people have with each other. Should the government provide affordable housing for low-income families? Should parks and playgrounds be built and maintained collectively for all to enjoy? Deeply embedded in public planning is the assumption that people are dependent on each other in innumerable and substantive ways that require public attention, an assertion that rubs against the individualism that anchors both liberal democracy and capitalism.

Planning theorists are those scholars whose primary concern is this interplay of the technical, political, and moral issues that circulate through the various initiatives of democratic governments. Specifically, their world is the world of urban and regional planning. As theorists, they strive to articulate the intellectual foundations of public planning and, on that basis, formulate appropriate ways to plan effectively. They develop their thoughts by reflecting on what planners do using the lenses of the social sciences, the natural sciences, and political philosophy. For the most part, their goal is not to explain how and why planning is actually done, but to indicate to practicing planners what they *should* be doing so that cities and regions can prosper and people can live well in a just and democratic world. Normative theory, not positive theory, is what dominates.[1] Moreover, the interests of planning theorists are both scholarly and practical: they want their ideas to be recognized by their academic colleagues, absorbed by the students who sit attentively in their classrooms, and adopted by practitioners.

This book is about that body of literature known as planning theory. It is written for graduate students in urban and regional planning who wish to learn more about the field's intellectual foundations, for planning scholars who wish to deepen and broaden their understanding of how planning is meant to be done, for professionals who want to reflect on what it is they do, and for those curious "outsiders" who want to know what it means to plan. My goal is to introduce the reader to the issues that planning theorists find compelling. No definitive list of these issues exists, of course. From the beginning, planning theorists have disagreed on what aspects of planning matter and, consequently, on what theoretical perspectives are most appropriate: the literature is both thematically diverse and contentious. Yet, a few theories have become widely adopted, with one particular set of approaches – those centered on rationality – having endured for decades. Given the multitude of ways that planning can be achieved and the many meanings that can be attached to it, the variety of theoretical interventions is unsurprising.

In order to navigate this unruly terrain, I focus on four general and core tasks – knowing, engaging, prescribing, and executing – and devote a chapter to each. Admittedly, these tasks are not exclusive to planning: dentistry and civil engineering could be described in a similar way. What matters is how they are interpreted in relation to the way planning is practiced and understood. Before delving further into this scheme, however, I need to set planning theory within its professional and academic home of urban and regional planning, establish the intellectual foundations on which planning theories are built, and introduce the reader to planning theory's various strands.

1.1   Urban and regional planning

Planning theorists are found almost solely in one realm of planning. Despite the many settings in which planning occurs – from homes to insurance companies to professional sports franchises – and the assortment of academic and professional fields in which it is relevant, only urban and regional planning has spawned a project devoted to theoretical self-understanding. Business schools might assign a faculty member to teach strategic planning, a public health program might require knowledge of family planning, and an economics department might offer a course on comparative economic systems from free markets to central planning, but only in academic programs of urban and regional planning do we find a distinct group of educators who claim to be planning theorists. And, even though the profession of planning has been around for more than a century, planning theorists are a recent phenomenon – a product of the mid-20th century.

Urban and regional planning took an institutionalized form with the emergence of the industrial cities in the late 19th century. The many social and environmental problems engendered and the subsequent efforts of local governments to ameliorate them soon gave rise to a planning profession. Yet, the physical planning that dominates the field can be traced back centuries. Consider the reign of the Egyptian pharaohs, the agricultural settlements of the Euphrates Valley, and the Ming Dynasty in China. The pyramids, vast irrigation systems, and the Great Wall – the large-scale projects of these societies – could not have been realized without foresight and without the coordination of labor and resources associated with planning. More closely aligned with contemporary planning are the towns constructed during the expansion of the Roman empire, when settlements and military camps were organized with central plazas, fortifications, and lineal streets. Today, most people equate urban planning with the spatial arrangement of streets and buildings, public squares, railroad stations, homes, and marketplaces.

Most important for the history of the profession is the period spanning the 19th and early 20th centuries when the Industrial Revolution and the urbanization that it spawned led to numerous efforts to address the consequences attendant to large, chaotic, and seemingly unmanageable cities (Hall 2002; Ward 2002). English reformers proposed "garden cities" in the countryside as an alternative to living in polluted, crowded, and unhealthy London. Factory owners built communities for their workers in Bourneville in England and Pullman (Illinois) and Hershey (Pennsylvania) in the United States. Later, in Italy, during the 1920s, Mussolini established new towns in rural areas to release urban population pressure and strengthen an agriculture sector depleted by migration to the cities. A decade later Stalin in the Soviet Union embraced a similar initiative that expanded and decentralized heavy manufacturing to avoid the problems that characterized big, industrial cities. After World War II, Germany, Japan, and Poland launched major rebuilding initiatives in cities that had been severely damaged during the war. Around the world, governments developed new highway systems, hydroelectric plants, telecommunication networks, and water supply systems. All required planning.

Beginning in the early 20th century, local governments established planning agencies and staffed them with professionally trained planners knowledgeable about how to manage growth and anticipate future development. Supporting them were reformers, mainly women, who operated settlement houses for immigrants and the native poor and engaged in urban beautification projects (Spain 2001). Soon thereafter, these embryonic planners turned to rationalizing street systems and regulating land uses. Planning was also extended to the provision of parks and playgrounds, the building of social housing, the placement and extension of water and sewage systems, the protection of air and water quality, the location of public facilities such as swimming pools and community centers, and (in the United States and England) the redevelopment of downtown areas that had become derelict due to the flight of manufacturing industries and businesses and the in-migration and segregation of poor, marginalized, and often racialized groups.

Around this time, and in response to the demand for planning experts, a small number of universities began to offer educational programs in city and regional planning (Perloff 1957). These programs were established in schools of architecture. There, planning was envisioned as a physical or spatial planning that involved the functional and aesthetic arrangement of buildings and activities. Architect–planners were trained in landscape design, civil engineering, and housing. Following World War II, and more so in the United States than in other parts of the world, planning educators incorporated ideas from the social sciences and began to distance planning education from architectural education. Planning became primarily associated with local development and the built environment and its prominence in the administration of the economy, large bureaucracies, major infrastructural projects, corporate management, and social welfare policy was lost to planning theorists. Academic programs of planning narrowly addressed cities, regions, and neighborhoods, while other forms of planning – and theorizing about them – were left to those enrolled in business schools, management programs, and civil engineering departments.

After the 1950s, planning educators with academic aspirations – in contrast to those who were primarily practitioners – turned their attention to the field's intellectual credentials (Sarbib 1983; Taylor 1998). They asked what was essential to planning and what distinguished it as an applied social science. They hoped that providing answers to these questions would enable planning to attain scholarly status in the university and bring cohesion to what they believed to be an intellectually weak, educational project. These nascent planning theorists turned to ideas developed by the Scottish polymath Patrick Geddes in the late 19th and early 20th centuries that formalized what it meant to plan. Geddes proposed a three-step process of survey, analysis, and design – "diagnosis before treatment" – in which planners would first survey the region being planned to develop a detailed knowledge of its landscape, geology, historical sites, and productive activities and then study (analysis) this knowledge to establish the basis for a regional plan (design). In fact, much of what might be considered early planning theory involved reflection on the nature of the plan and of planmaking (Batty and Marshall 2009, 560; Van der Goot and Simey 1949). Geddes's scheme also fit neatly with an emerging "systems analysis" that was increasingly part of governmental policymaking, budgeting, and military affairs. When combined with a postwar sense of efficacy and a fascination with science and technology, planning thought gave birth to a rational-comprehensive model of planning in which planners focused on the collection and analysis of data as a basis for identifying the most appropriate course of action for a given set of goals and conditions.

In the United States, one of the earliest writings on planning theory came from two professors, Paul Davidoff and Thomas Reiner. In their 1962 article (Davidoff and Reiner 1962), they proposed that the core task of planning was the determination of appropriate futures through the generation and management of choices. In presenting their argument, Davidoff and Reiner built on the work of John Dyckman, a professor at the University of California: Berkeley, who in 1960 had circulated an unpublished piece that he titled "Introduction to Readings in the Theory of Planning." A year later, he published "Planning and Decision Theory" (Dyckman 1961) in which he claimed that planning was a form of decision-making that served as an alternative to markets and politics and whose essence was best captured by the normative rather than the behavioral aspects of decision theory. Despite these efforts, the U.S. planning scholars John Friedmann and Barclay Hudson (1974, 13) would write in 1974 that "planning cannot presently claim to be sustained by a coherent body of theoretical propositions."[2]

Nevertheless, and with these writings providing impetus, planning theorists began to explore numerous pathways that might reveal the ideas on which planning and its practice were based. Some theorists turned to democratic theory to call for a planning that was participatory, while others drew on a neo-Marxist political economy to launch a critique of the capitalist state and its planning function. Still others read deeply into the communicative action theory developed by the German philosopher Jürgen Habermas and proposed a planning that was less about analyzing data than speaking truthfully to and learning from others. Subsequently, a number of theorists took the notion of participation and reframed it around collaboration and mutual learning. In developing their approaches, these theorists adopted and adapted ideas from such intellectuals outside the field as Michel Foucault, John Dewey, Hannah Arendt, Bruno Latour, and Iris Young as well as from such theoretical perspectives as feminist theory, postmodernism, and pragmatism.

Today, planning theory is ubiquitous in planning education and considered (at least by theorists) to be as indispensable to planning students as knowledge of land markets, ecological systems, statistics, and government. Planners are meant to be more than experts in a substantive planning area; they should also be able to devise ways to address problems, exploit opportunities, and work with non-planners to arrive at agreement on what should be done. To do this, theorists argue, practitioners need to reflect on how they plan; this is the only way that planning can become effective, just, and democratic. One of the goals of planning theory is to guide practice.

Within planning education, then, a small group of scholars is committed to exploring what it means to plan. Less concerned with the technical aspects, their focus is mainly on political, social, and moral issues. Their hope is that planning theory will become part of the "knowing-in-practice" that shapes the decisions of practitioners (Schön 1982). In this sense, and given its normative thrust, planning theorists serve as the profession's self-appointed conscience. The attachment they have inward to the university, however, overshadows their orientation outward to the profession. Planning theory, for the most part, is meant to be the intellectual project of planning education. It is the project that confers scholarly credibility within higher education where the traditional disciplines still rule and where the pursuit of knowledge (and not simply the vocational training of students) is most highly valued (Beauregard 2015, 192–210). To this extent, planning theory is not just about planning practice.

1.2 Intellectual foundations

Given their academic leanings, it should be of little surprise that planning theorists position themselves within the same intellectual realm as that of the academic disciplines they hope to emulate. Their work is deeply rooted in European Enlightenment thought and committed to the values – rationality, progress, science, democracy, and reform – associated with modernity.[3]

Planning is one consequence of the belief that the world can be known and that knowledge can be used to act intentionally and, thus, with purpose. By definition, the actions of an enlightened person are based on and justified by reasons that lead to the intended outcomes. The planner attempts to align actions with previously established goals. Free of prejudices, religious strictures, and superstitions, she additionally proceeds on the basis of experience, with that experience subsequently filtered through scientific procedures that turn evidence into facts. This way of thinking about the world has led theorists to situate a particular type of rationality at the core of planning. Planning is meant to be functionally or instrumentally rational, connecting means to ends and actions to goals. Planners are thus encouraged to think of themselves as technical experts who have substantive knowledge of the workings of cities and regions.

Acting rationally and scientifically creates the potential for bringing progress to human affairs. Within planning, this is reflected in a reformist impulse that aims to improve how people live, work, and play. This impulse is what gave rise in the early 20th century to a planning embraced by government and also what explains, in part, the normative inclination of planning theorists. If it were impossible to better organize how people live together, how cities and regions are arranged, and how large-scale projects are implemented, there would be no need for planning.

The embrace of rationality also signals a commitment to separating science from politics and a belief in an objectivity unpolluted by political calculation. In this form, the advice that planners give is what is best for the city or region and the people within it. The early city planners, though, soon realized that for them to be successful, government (the body that represents the public) would have to be democratic and made rational – a task known as municipal reform. Doing so would isolate the effects of politics-as-usual from the planning and management of the city.

Planning's reform impulse brought forth another legacy of the Enlightenment, the belief in the inherent value of the individual and a commitment to equality. Early on, and in most but not all countries, planners associated themselves with liberalism and democracy. (The Soviet Union was one exception.) Planners would be those experts who advised popularly elected governmental officials. In this role, they would represent the public interest (i.e., speak for the people as a whole) and be an antidote to special interests and narrow political agendas. Expertise and democracy were assumed to be compatible. In democratic settings, the impulse to control and regulate the decisions of businesses and households was given a liberal cast and, in that form, became part of both early 20th-century reform movements and the welfare states of the mid-20th century. Today, and with few exceptions, practitioners and theorists alike champion democratic processes and equality of outcomes.

Throughout its history, and particularly in liberal democracies, the reform impulse has pitted governmental planning against capitalism. Profit-driven landlords and factory owners, for example, were deemed responsible for the slum conditions and labor exploitation of the industrial city era. Today, oil refineries and coal-powered electrical plants are sources of environmental problems. The capitalist system seems to work in ways that harm some groups of people and not others, that create the super-rich and the desperately poor, and that enable some cities to prosper while others decay. Nonetheless, the early planners in England, Germany, and the United States did not call for replacing capitalism with, for example, socialism. (And, neither do contemporary planners.) Rather, and in democratic settings, planning has become a public-regarding activity and is meant to hold in check the undesirable consequences of development and "mop up" after capitalism's excesses without dampening capitalism's ability to generate growth and progress.

Of all these Enlightenment values, arguably the most central for planning is rationality. Whether cast in terms of the importance of empirical evidence to decision-making or the positioning of goals prior to action, the early planning theorists placed functional and technical rationality at the center of their theoretical musings. Planning was seen as bringing rational thought to human affairs and meant to be free of political calculation. Led by experts, an unruly world would be disciplined and governments would carry out public projects ranging from the proper location for new schools to the building of national highway networks. Much like planning itself, these claims were themselves normative, not inherent to planning and without which it could not exist, but rather universal and thus without context and history. Planning theorists set themselves the task of trying to understand what these different values meant, how they shaped the way planning was done, and whether other values would contribute to a better planning.

1.3   Theories of planning

This Enlightenment and modernist perspective was crystallized in the rational-comprehensive model, an explicitly normative approach to how planning should be done (Banfield 1959). The model is often stylized around a logical sequence of tasks: analyze the conditions requiring intervention, establish goals, list all the alternative means for realizing those goals, develop procedures for assessing the consequences of each of the alternatives, rank the alternatives on the basis of their consequences and thus relevance to the goal, and, finally, select the "best" course of action. In carrying out these procedures, planners are to consider all possible alternatives and all likely consequences. Nothing is to be overlooked. To do otherwise would be insensitive to the original goal and run the risk of identifying an inferior array of possibilities. In effect, planners should be comprehensive as well as rational. Few planning theorists, though, have claimed that the sequence is inviolable or that individual tasks are unproblematic. Rather, the rational-comprehensive model is meant to be an ideal toward which planners strive.

From the start, the model had its critics. The U.S. management theorist Herbert Simon pointed out that the demands made on the planner went well beyond the limited rationality of human beings and that the decision-maker should aim for a satisfactory solution (what he labeled "satisficing") rather than an optimal one. The American political scientist Charles Lindblom (1959) argued that the rational-comprehensive model was absent from the world of policymaking. Instead, policy-makers "muddled through": decision-making was incremental not synoptic. And, from the same disciplinary and national perspective, Aaron Wildavsky (1973) claimed that the whole idea of a rational planning was so vague and ill-defined as to be simply non-existent, while Horst Rittel and Melvin Webber (1973), two U.S. theorists less dismissive of planning, pointed out that the kinds of issues that confronted planners were, in fact, "wicked problems" immune to rational techniques and that rational procedures were of little use in these situations.

In response to these and other criticisms, adherents of the approach offered modifications and searched for ways to retain the model's core ideas (Faludi 1973). In 1956, the U.S. planning scholar Martin Meyerson reworked the rational-comprehensive model to better position it between long-range comprehensive planning meant to guide development and the immediate decisions involved in implementing a plan. For him, planners needed to operate in the "middle-range." (Importantly for theorists, he called for a professionalization of planning that would involve "being self-conscious about our work activity" (Meyerson 1956, 58).) Another of these variations was strategic planning. Borrowed from organizational theory, strategic planning dispenses with the demands for full knowledge and linear processes and instead proposes a more dynamic and grounded interplay of decisions arrayed around environmental scanning, visioning, implementation, and evaluation. Of particular concern are the strengths and weaknesses of and opportunities and threats faced by an issue's stakeholders.

The rational-comprehensive model and its variations came under even less friendly criticism. For many on the political left, the social turmoil of the 1950s and 1960s suggested that planning and policymaking based on a rationality grounded in expertise were undemocratic and mainly used to serve the technical needs of those in power. In short, the model was not just infeasible, but morally bankrupt and oblivious to its own politics. The world was riddled with conflict and the idea of the public interest was more ideological than not. Planners and planning theorists had to recognize the political nature of planning and the social fragmentation of society. What was needed was a democratic planning. This gave rise to proposals for an advocacy planning in which, according to Paul Davidoff (1965), its major proponent, planners would align with groups outside the state that lack access to planning expertise and, in that relationship, advocate for their interests against that of the government. Later, Norman Krumholz (1982), once the head of the city planning agency in Cleveland (U.S.A.), proposed an equity planning model in which governmental planners would attempt to maximize the choices available to those on society's margins. Attention was shifted from the analytical role of the planner to his political role, with planning theory becoming less about solving the problem of how to justify planning from a technical point of view and more about how to act democratically. Reinforcing this politicization of planning were those scholars who took to neo-Marxism with its emphasis on the capitalist roots of urban problems, the tendency of the state to serve the interests of capital, and the need for organizing not just the workers but the poor and marginalized as well (Fainstein and Fainstein 1979; Roweis 1981).

With the recognition that success at planning was as much a function of political relationships as analysis and expertise, planning theorists began to explore planning as a social activity involving affiliations between planners and non-planners. In retrospect, this was the major challenge to the rational-comprehensive model. These new theoretical initiatives emphasized the need for transparent and honest communication, listening, joint fact-finding, and inclusivity. With more women and even a few minorities entering as students and professors, the planning academy and planning practice were becoming more diverse. With consensus less easily assumed, planning had to become more sensitive to alternative points of view. These new theories were also compatible with the earlier-proposed advocacy planning. Communicative planning and collaboration were tools that could be used to address inequalities and do so democratically. Communicative planning, moreover, fit well with the 1980s postmodern concern with discourse. Postmodernism and collaborative planning aligned with an emerging feminism to allow the voices of women and others on the margins of society to be heard.

Neo-Marxists challenged the communicative planning and collaborative planning theorists. They argued that the latter were too narrowly focused on process to the detriment of planning's substantive consequences. The U.S. theorist Susan Fainstein (2005a, 121), one of the leading commentators on this substance–process divide, commented that "much of planning theory discusses what planners do with little reference either to the consequential constraints under which they do it or the object they seek to effect." There was no guarantee, she and others claimed, that democratic collaboration and deliberative engagement would lead to an erasure of social inequalities. Needed was a "just-city" planning that reduced disparities in access to affordable and quality housing, public services, employment, and health care. People had a "right to the city" that involved living well and the task of the planners was to work toward its realization.[4]

To make sense of these various strands of planning theory, a number of planning scholars have endeavored to organize different planning theories within a single, overarching, conceptual framework (e.g., Dubrucká (2016) and Lim (1986)). One of the most ambitious of these attempts, and the only one I know that extends beyond urban and regional planning, is John Friedmann's *Planning in the Public Domain* published in 1987. In this book, Friedmann, one of the field's major figures, considered the intellectual history of American planning since the 18th century. He positioned planning at the intersection of reason and democracy, where it has strived to link existing conditions to future possibilities. His is an inclusive sense of planning centered on collective action involving states and/or civil society and always occurring in the public realm. Drawing from sociology, neoclassical economics, organization development, historical materialism, pragmatism, and systems analysis among other intellectual fields, Friedmann developed a typology consisting of four different approaches to planning: policy analysis, social learning, social mobilization, and social reform.

Policy analysis is anchored in scientific rationality and is meant to advise state policymaking. Its origins were in the early post-World War II period, years when technology and science came to be viewed as the keys to human progress. Social learning is concerned with the acquisition of knowledge in organizational and political settings and occurs outside the state rather than within it. Friedmann associates this approach with the American philosopher John Dewey. Social mobilization focuses on such collective action as labor activism, utopian communities, and anarchistic movements, and takes place outside the state. The last approach, social reform, is directed at identifying social problems and devising solutions that can be implemented either by the state or reformist movements. Its roots, Friedmann tells us, are in France in the early 19th century with Henri de Saint-Simon and other utopian thinkers. Of the four types, policy analysis and social reform are the most closely aligned with mainstream, urban and regional planning.

Rejecting Friedmann's wide perspective, the Israeli scholar Oren Yiftachel (1989) proposed that the plurality of planning theories can be fitted into three categories: analytical, urban form, and procedural. Analytical theories reflect on how planning is done in various socio-political settings. It includes both Weberian analysis and managerialism as well as the reformist inclination to functional and technical rationality. Planning theories of urban form concentrate on the physical manifestation of planning and are closely related to its architectural heritage. Here, issues of decentralization, renewal, and master plans are paramount while intellectual theories from outside planning are absent. Theories of urban form are considered substantive theories. Lastly, procedural theories focus on the sequence of activities that comprise the planning process. They include attention to design methodology, rational pragmatism, systems analysis, and advocacy. Pivotal for Yiftachel's typology is the distinction between theories of urban form and theories of the planning process; the first focuses on the substantive consequences of planning (e.g., social housing) and the second on the tasks in which planners engage. Yiftachel further acknowledged that planning theories can be either explanatory or prescriptive. This is essentially a distinction between positive theories meant to expose how things work and normative theories meant to direct our gaze to what should be done.

Philip Allmendinger (2002a; 2002b; 2009), a U.K. planning professor, also distinguished between substantive and procedural theories. Procedural theories are divided into those that are developmental (i.e., supportive of current socio-political relationships even though committed to reform) and those that are oppositional (such as Marxist political economy) and view public problems as embedded in prevailing socio-political arrangements that need to be changed. The distinction that most interests him is that between procedural theories of the past (all of which he views as positivist) and theories "after" positivism. The latter theories consider positivism's fact–value dichotomy to be false, embrace a non-linear conception of time thereby rejecting a determinative notion of progress, and set planning in its spatial and temporal context. As a framework for making sense of various theoretical positions, Allmendinger proposes a post-positivist typology that consists of five theoretical approaches: framing theories (i.e., worldviews), exogenous theories (e.g., theories of democracy), social theories (e.g., Marxism), social scientific philosophical understandings (e.g., public choice theory), and indigenous planning theory. What is important here is his rejection of the substance–process distinction and, similar to Friedmann and Yiftachel, his acknowledgement of the variety of ways planning theory might be conceived and the multitude of intellectual resources on which it draws.

1.4   Core tasks

Instead of describing these theories one by one in chronological fashion or devising another typology, I propose a framework that brings planning theory's central themes to the surface. The idea is to cut across the various theories by emphasizing the core tasks that planners have to perform in order to make planning happen. This focus on practice echoes the Marxist notion of praxis (i.e., actions necessary to change society) as well as theories developed in the fields of education and organization theory that link practice to social learning. A connection can also be made to theories of action found in the social sciences, specifically those focused on agency (Beauregard 2015, 42–49). The concern of all these approaches is the interactions among people working together to realize a common project. To this extent, theories of practice are built up from social relationships rather than drawn down from overarching structures.

Presenting planning theory in this way privileges process over consequences, thereby casting planning theory as much more procedural than substantive (as these theorists understand the distinction) (Camhis 1979, 2–7). In fact, and moreover, almost all planning theories take planning practice (rather than the city) as their object. Few theorists reflect on planning as an idea (as did John Friedmann) or planning as a mode of institutional organization equivalent to, yet distinct from, markets or politics. In a similar fashion, I de-emphasize the structural forces (e.g., globalization) and historical conditions (e.g., the rise of nationalism) that shaped and continue to shape planning. My scheme privileges practice.

As an example of a similar approach, consider an article by the U.K. planning theorist Simin Davoudi (2015) titled "Planning as Practice of Knowing." In it, she defines planning as a process of knowing and learning in which planners use their expertise, experience, and reading of social situations to make practical judgments. What allows planners to act as planners is knowledge. Consequently, the core tasks for planners are knowing what to do, knowing how to do it, and knowing why it should be done (i.e., to what ends). These forms of knowing are the basis for doing planning. They are also the basis for being pragmatic and purposeful as well as for negotiating both disagreements and the institutional, organizational, and political relationships that mediate planning and what it can achieve.

My framework for discussing planning theories, then, is practice based and task oriented. Planning practice, I argue, can be characterized in terms of four core tasks: knowing, engaging, prescribing, and executing. Admittedly, these tasks are not peculiar to planning; they are common to many activities. One can easily imagine an architect or a political advisor attending to each and all of them. Nonetheless, they are the intellectual problems facing planning theorists. That each task is quite general signals their malleability and enables planning theorists to interpret the tasks in a multitude of ways. Knowing means something different within the rational-comprehensive model with its roots in technical rationality to how it is treated by a theorist drawing from the ideas of Michel Foucault. Neither is each task meant to be mutually exclusive or so integral that it cannot be taken apart and distributed across the planning process. And, as a last caveat, the four tasks should not be considered as a sequence, with knowing preceding prescribing, for example. What I am proposing is a heuristic framework that enables us to compare and contrast the different planning theories and not a scheme for how to do planning.

First, as regards knowing, much discussion within planning theory has reflected on the relation of knowledge to action, that is, the extent to which planning advice and planning activities have to be based on particular ways of understanding the world. Generally accepted is that planning is evidence based and that planners can hardly act as planners without knowledge of the reality they hope to change. But what does this mean and what kinds of knowledge are appropriate? Is technical knowledge the key? If not, and if experiential knowledge is required, what does this mean for the science-based expertise of planners? More practically, must knowledge precede action or is action a prelude to knowledge? The task of knowing thus encompasses the conditions under which planning is necessary, appropriate, and effective. For planning theorists, these questions and issues have led to three concerns. First is the extent to which knowledge is required for planning to be realized as rational and intentional. Second is the types of knowledge that enable planners to be effective and/or democratic. If more than technical knowledge is required, then non-planners need to be involved and their local knowledge and experiences given value. This being the case, third is how these different knowledges should be brought together to influence what planners propose.

Planners' need "to know" and the concern to make planning democratic connects planners to the second task – engaging. When planning is being done, different forms of engagement occur: delegation, consultation, advice-giving, collaboration, negotiation. They can be put, conceptually at least, in two basic categories: performative engagements in which planners work with others to achieve professional goals and democratic engagements meant to foster a more inclusive planning. The latter is the most discussed in the planning theory literature with theorists mainly absorbed with communicative planning, collaboration, and pragmatism. No matter the theoretical approach, interpersonal relations (and not, say, social mobilization) constitute the pivot point of planning practice. Additionally, planning theorists treat engaging as solely involving humans, even though a few recognize that planners collaborate with non-human things (e.g., computer software) as well. With whom or what they engage, how they do so, and with what consequences are the issues that matter to the task of engaging.

The third task is prescribing. Haunting planning theorists and practitioners is the moral basis of planning or, less portentously, the extent to which planning is a normative activity and not solely or simply a technical task. Planning is always a matter of proposing what should be done. However, no technical path connects evidence to prescription. At the same time, planning embodies values and these values guide the proposals that planners develop and the advice they offer. Consequently, theorists have reflected on the moral responsibilities of planning and the extent to which planners should be guided by ethical principles. This concern with situated ethical judgments leads directly to politics and the use of ideologies and partisan choices to resolve the prescriptive dilemma which characterizes public decision-making. More specifically, the task of prescribing positions the planner morally and politically in relation to the growth and development of cities and regions and to marginalized and oppressed groups and the potential for their empowerment.

Executing – bringing about and making real the consequences that planners intend – is the fourth task. In planning, a distinction has always existed between planning and implementation, that is, between developing a plan for what needs to be done and actually doing it. In fact, planners are not the ones who carry out the plans that they have made. But do planners have responsibilities with regard to implementation? Can they overcome a semantic limitation that confines planning to that which precedes the taking of action? To what extent should planners become directly engaged in bringing about a better world? This might well mean moving away from technical and communicative rationality to a strategic rationality that entangles planners in power relations that they have traditionally derided and wish to avoid. If they do become so engaged, is the next step an insurgent planning launched from outside of government? In brief, how can and should planners pursue influence beyond planning itself?

Knowing, engaging, prescribing, and executing can be fruitfully treated as different theoretical issues. In practice, of course, they are not so distinct and often overlap, intersect, push against, and seep into each other. Additionally, they almost always confront planners all at once rather than in neat, sequential order. That these tasks have these qualities is one of the factors contributing to the unruliness of planning theory.

1.5   Postscript

To conclude this introductory chapter, I want to offer a few caveats. First, a comment on theory. For the most part, planning theories are closer to perspectives than to highly formal, analytic schemes. They are characterized by heuristics rather than hypotheses. And, as mentioned, they tend to be prescriptive: explanation is not their primary goal. And because planning theories are almost always normative, they are more concerned with possibilities than realities. Planning theories tend to be general guides to action rather than depictions of how or why planning happens as it does. That said, theorists are expected to take account of how planning occurs in practice.

Second, my focus is almost wholly on procedural theories of planning rather than substantive theories. This decision reflects the bias of my U.S. perspective as well as my social science (rather than architectural) inclinations. This procedural emphasis, as will be discussed, risks succumbing to a universality of timeless-ness and placeless-ness at odds with the current emphasis on linking planning theory to the material enactment – the situated-ness – of planning practice. Procedural theories also tend to ignore the fact that "major differences exist in the ways that planning is conceived, institutionalized, and carried out" (Friedmann 2005, 184) across such institutional and cultural contexts as nations (but see Harrison (2006) and Knieling and Othengraften (2009)).

Third, my discussion of these four core tasks draws wholly from the English-language literature. This does not necessarily confine the text to theorists from English-speaking countries: we will encounter many theorists for whom English is not their first language. It does mean that planning theorists who do not write in English are unrepresented. In fact, most of the theorists that I will reference come from the United States and the United Kingdom with fewer from Western Europe and Canada, and even fewer from Australia and South Africa (Huxley and Yiftachel 2000). Planning theory has mainly been an Anglo-American and Western European project. In short, it is of the global North.[5] To give a sense of the global breadth of planning theory, limited as it is, I have indicated the countries with which theorists are professionally associated, though not their nationalities of birth or education. This, of course, raises the difficult issue of how space and place influence one's theorizing, an issue that I will not address.

Fourth, I generally ignore the chronological relationship among the various theories, although this was briefly alluded to earlier in the chapter. I am less interested in the history of planning thought than in theoretical approaches to the core tasks. I also focus primarily on the major theoretical approaches: the rational-comprehensive model and its variants, advocacy planning, communicative action, collaborative planning, the just city, and insurgent planning. Less dominant theories are discussed, but I have not attempted to be exhaustive: there are just too many different issues to address and too many different ways to think about them. Numerous intellectual forays have been and continue to be undertaken, but many fewer have been widely adopted.

Finally, I imagined this book as a literature review, not as my idiosyncratic perspective on planning theory. (The interested reader can find this perspective in Beauregard (2015).) Then, as a way to counteract my intellectual biases and authorial presence (impossible to totally suppress), I have included quotations from numerous planning theorists. All intellectual projects are dialogues among a group of people with a shared interest. For this particular dialogue to be appreciated, we need to hear from the individuals involved. Still, my intention was not to include every transient idea or every person who ever wrote or published on planning theory; neither was it to privilege the most prominent of them. Nor do I track, with rare exceptions, planning ideas to their intellectual roots. This keeps the focus on the planning theory literature. My objective is to present a coherent and informative perspective on planning theory as seen through the lens of four core tasks: knowing, engaging, prescribing, and executing.

NOTES

1 The American planning theorist Britton Harris (1997, 483) wrote that "the theory of a profession is of necessity a normative theory." Also by necessity, this entails recognizing how practice is done (Dalton 1989).

2 It is difficult to date the origins of planning theory. One of the earliest writings seems to be a sociological approach proposed in 1949 by Van der Goot and Simey (1949). I would also include Banfield (1959), Glass (1959), Lindblom (1959), and Meyerson (1956) as part of the foundational, contemporary literature.

3 Of course, neither the Enlightenment nor modernity were or have been internally consistent or invariant across time or cultures. I use the concepts mainly as framing devices.

4 Despite decades of criticism and alternative approaches, rationality still remains important to many planning theorists. See Archibugi (2007) and the many writings of Andreas Faludi and Ernest Alexander.

5 A robust engagement with planning theory does seem to be underway in China (Cao and Hillier 2013).

2   Knowing

Planning is not meant to be intuitive. Its theorists do not expect it to happen in a subconscious way. To cast it in these terms would narrow good planning to a few random individuals and make it effectively unteachable. Neither do theorists think of planning as spontaneous. Rather, planners are expected to be both thoughtful and cautious. Before any planning is done, there has to be a pause. Planners must hesitate. During this time, their task is to gather information, carefully consider its implications, and reflect on how to proceed. Without this pause and the knowledge to which it gives rise, planners are immobilized. An uncontemplated action is one that is spontaneous, intuitive, or desperate. To plan in the world, planners must first know the world. Knowledge is what enables planners to carry out their intentions and "those who write about planning theory," the British theorist Heather Campbell (2012, 137) has remarked, "are essentially writing about the nature, role, and (mis)use of knowledge."

Knowing is thus essential to planning, and, almost without exception, theorists are fixated on the place of knowledge in planning practice. In their well-cited article from the early 1970s, aptly titled "Knowledge and Action: A Guide to Planning Theory," John Friedmann and Barclay Hudson claimed that planning is "an activity centrally connected with the *linkage between knowledge and organized action*" (1974, 2, emphasis in original). More recently, Simin Davoudi (2015) has made "knowing" central to planning. She casts planning as a process dominated by knowing such that every step is a matter of gathering, analyzing, and critiquing knowledge in the pursuit of practical judgments. Unlike Friedmann and Hudson, however, Davoudi problematizes knowledge: it is not one thing – and obvious – but situated, provisional, mediated, and contested.

Davoudi's theoretical stance reflects the thinking two decades earlier of the Australian (now Canadian) planning theorist Leonie Sandercock (1998). In her work, Sandercock conceived of planning as gripped by an Enlightenment epistemology that privileges science, objectivity, and "an individualistic, rationalist, secularist belief in progress" (p. 61). Deeming this socially and politically narrow as well as culturally exclusionary, her theoretical task, as she saw it, was to reposition planning theory in an epistemology that acknowledged a multiplicity of people and perspectives and that opened planning to feminist, postcolonial, racialized, and postmodern experiences. For both Davoudi and Sandercock, the linkage between knowledge and organized action requires a critique of knowledge itself. Planning knowledge is not meant to be solely instrumental and scientific. Technical knowledge is central to planning practice and of theoretical importance, but, alone, it is insufficient.

Despite the attention it has attracted, the relationship between knowledge and action within planning theory remains unresolved. Widely accepted is that knowledge does not simply precede action. It does not justify what planners do, only to be set aside as action occurs. For theorists of the rational-comprehensive model, this seemed to be precisely its function. Nothing was to be done until knowing was complete. Contrarily, critics have proposed that isolating knowledge early in the planning process and confining planners to technical knowledge and instrumental rationality are incompatible with planning in liberal, multicultural democracies. This has led them to consider other types of knowledge, other "knowers," and other places where planning knowledge might be situated. Knowledge became valued for reasons other than its content and scientific legitimacy. It was recast as constructed in social relations rather than discovered in a real world of facts, with the act of knowing being of as much value as what is known.

This critical approach situates planning in democratic deliberations and unearths new ways to think about knowing and knowledge. Rather than solely scientific and evidence-based, planning knowledge is envisioned as experiential, gendered, and co-produced. Persuasion, mutual deliberation, and storytelling supplement or even replace technical exposition. Not only social and cultural differences matter but geopolitical divisions as well. Greater attention is paid to the origins of planning knowledge in the global North and its deeply problematic application to conditions in the global South. In short, how planners know, what knowledge is appropriate, and whose knowledge matters have become central themes in the knowledge–action debate (Connell 2010).[1]

2.1   Technical knowledge

In the ideal version of the rational-comprehensive model, the field's foundational theoretical approach, knowledge is essential for defining a condition, identifying and assessing possible interventions, evaluating interventions in terms of their ability to achieve the intended goals, and predicting whether the actions that follow will be effective. At each step, planners draw on their specialized knowledge of how neighborhoods, cities, and regions produce jobs, housing, and open space; how governments are able to provide public services; and how these functional relationships can be manipulated to diminish air pollution, prevent slums, make elementary schools accessible to children, and minimize the time spent by workers traveling to and from their place of employment. Technical data on population shifts, highway congestion, housing quality, and resident access to parks and playgrounds have to be gathered and analyzed in order to stipulate what needs to be done and what interventions are most likely to succeed. Governmental censuses have to be consulted and surveys undertaken and then rates of change calculated, flood plains mapped, and geographical information systems mobilized.

Rational-comprehensive approaches are heavily reliant on what is called theories-in-planning, that is, theories that explain residential choice or identify the factors governing wetland restoration. These theories are different from theories-of-planning which focus on the planning process. Theories-in-planning address the "what," "how," and "why" questions of knowledge. They explain what housing markets are and how they work, why people choose automobiles over mass transit, and why neighborhoods decline. What they do not explain is how we arrive at this knowledge and, then, how to intervene in these processes. Unaddressed by theories-in-planning is the question of what the planner needs to do to take advantage of opportunities or remove undesirable conditions. The purpose of theories-of-planning is to link substantive knowledge with action.

In the 1960s and 1970s, one of the most important of these theories-in-planning was systems analysis and various analytical techniques associated with it such as computer modeling, linear programming, and cost–benefit analysis. (The more recent version of this is data analytics, also known as "big data" (Chadwick 1971).) The promise of these approaches is that we can know the world through the scientific analysis of large amounts of quantitative data. The world and its many sub-worlds are treated as complex, adaptive systems composed of an array of functionally interrelated parts either working in harmony or having fallen into disequilibrium. To understand how, say, a regional transportation network is operating, the planner has to identify its components and track (or model) the interactions that move people and goods around and beyond the region. In effect, planners know the world when they discover the logics that enable a system (or subsystem) to function. This knowing rests on the meta-theory of systems analysis and a particular theory-in-planning.

Systems analysis and other rational-comprehensive approaches also imagine a specific type of planner: a technical expert who draws conclusions and develops advice based on the analysis of scientific evidence (Mazza 1995). This planner has detailed and extensive knowledge of cities and regions and a set of tools for collecting and making sense of data. In addition, she has theoretical understandings – theories-in-planning – that enable her to explain why it is that a neighborhood has become distressed, why building highways along certain paths will decrease travel times and increase accessibility, and how governmental subsidies might encourage developers to build low-cost housing.

Planners, as experts, engage in the systematic identification, collection, analysis, and interpretation of data, what is commonly termed research. Practicing planners are always hungry for information: scouring government censuses, undertaking neighborhood surveys, and counting traffic flows on busy streets. Their academic counterparts perform systematic research on housing, community development, transportation, and land-use management (Sanchez and Afzalan 2018), all topics related to the legislation and regulations that govern planning. Once the planner, through research, has discovered the functional interdependencies that shape the development of cities and regions and how they play out in a specific situation, all that remains is to select an intervention that fits that logic and the analysis that supports it. Stated bluntly, knowing occurs before acting, not during it and certainly not after it. Implied is that once a plan is implemented, learning ceases. Even those who espouse such an approach, however, would have a difficult time defending that position. Nonetheless, putting knowing after action poses serious challenges to the integrity of the rational-comprehensive model.

Expert knowledge and scientific theories are thus central to how rational planning is to be done. The implication is that knowing is situated in the planner. The expert has the knowledge necessary for planning to happen and this is what makes her advice legitimate in the eyes of elected officials and the public. This is the way the city works, the rational planner states unequivocally: here is where the problem lies, and this is what should be done if you want the problem to disappear.

The planner, though, is meant to be more than an expert trafficking in esoteric knowledge. She should be, as the American planning scholar Harvey Perloff (1957) observed, a generalist with a specialty. That is, she should have a broad understanding of cities and regions along with deep knowledge of a specific area of planning practice. This combination enables the planner to act in relation to practical problems while also grasping how a particular planning intervention is connected to everything else that is happening in the city. Without specific knowledge, the planner cannot be effective. Without general knowledge, she cannot comprehend how planning interventions fit into and impinge on the city's complex web of relationships. Implicit is that this generalist with a specialty is in the best position to coordinate development activities, a claim to be taken up in the next chapter.

Still, the expert is not the decision-maker: others decide what to do. In fact, one cannot inhabit the expert role without a corresponding client. For governmental planners, the client is elected officials and the role of planners is to reduce the uncertainty facing them so that they can respond efficiently and effectively both to problems and to opportunities (Benveniste 1977). Decision-makers lack the technical knowledge of planners and cannot be expected to know what the consequences will be, for example, of only allowing manufacturing in certain parts of the city. Nor do they know how to be proactive in influencing where factories should best be located. They need experts to tell them. This means that planners' influence as well as their legitimacy in the eyes of elected officials and the public stems from the relevance of their recommendations. To the extent that their advice can be acted on and, when followed, achieves its intended consequences, planners are valued. Analysis – knowing about cities and regions and what governments are capable of doing – is what enables them to give that advice.

For governmental planners, the client – elected officials – also establishes the goals which guide planners in their work. Planners might monitor the city for emerging problems related to shrinking industrial districts or river pollution, but for them to act they need the officials to name a task and set a goal. Having a goal enables planners to be both intentional and functionally rational. In effect, expert-based planning theories divide the world into science and politics. Planners occupy the first realm and elected officials the second. This has the further effect of separating facts from values and thereby distinguishing ends from means. The result confines planners to means analysis, that is, to being instrumentally rational. The benefit of this for rational-comprehensive theorists is that it removes the difficult issues of politics and values from the planning process. When politics and values are placed outside of and precede planning, planners can suppress their values and believe that they act objectively. A political decision triggers planning, not a planning decision based on knowledge of a world gone awry or an emerging opportunity. In the end, politicians decide whether or not to implement the advice that they receive. That the client might not select the option that planners deem best is discouraging, but it is not something over which planners have (or should have) any influence, at least according to these theories. This is democracy in action. In short, planners should not become political. Planning is to remain thoroughly rational in a technical and instrumental sense and the task before the theorist is to understand the ways it can be made more effective through greater knowledge, more systematic analysis, and better advice.

2.2   Criticisms and alternatives

Even as these rational-comprehensive theories were being developed in the early postwar decades, critics began to question the scientific way of knowing they espoused and the emphasis they placed on expertise. The criticisms focused on the knowledge demands being made on the planner, the exclusive emphasis on technical knowledge, and the context-free bias that ignored diverse understandings critical for planning to be effective. Many of these criticisms came from within the rational-comprehensive model community; many others came from theorists who were staking out alternative theoretical approaches.

One of the major internal criticisms was made by Herbert Simon, who noted that rational models assumed that planners had an unlimited ability to absorb information, compute data, and interpret results. Contrarily, he claimed that all planners – all people in fact – have bounded rationality; that is, they can manage only limited amounts of information at any one time. And, although one might argue that computers could compensate for this deficiency, the resultant calculations still posed a cognitive challenge, not the least of which was that they had to be explained and translated into advice, something computers could not do. Simon further pointed out that people adjust to their bounded rationality by avoiding the pursuit of optimal solutions to problems. Most people aim for solutions that alleviate (rather than eliminate) the problem or that realize an objective within time and resource constraints. In effect, he famously wrote, they look for satisfactory solutions or, in his neologism, they "satisfice."

A similar critique came from decision theorists, who noted that the rational-comprehensive model posed an endless task when it asked planners to thoroughly define the problem, account for all possible responses, and assess every response against all possible objectives and conditions. The model had no stopping rules. It did not tell the planner when it was time to cease pursuing knowledge and, instead, frame their advice. In the real world and at some point, research has to stop and action has to be taken. In effect, critics observed, knowing so dominated the rational-comprehensive model that it seemed to be its sole purpose. Research became a fetish. In a world where the timeliness of what people do is often critical, such rational approaches are unhelpful.

Both bounded rationality and time and resource constraints imply that planning always occurs under conditions of uncertainty (Beauregard, forthcoming; Christensen 1985). Planners are poor predictors of the future, never fully cognizant of the consequences that their plans will engender, and are often inattentive to unintended outcomes. Much is unknown about the city, about the efficacy of potential actions, about the ways in which property owners, developers, and residents will respond to new regulations, and about the extent to which people will avoid or challenge what planners have proposed. Uncertainty is unavoidable and this is a sign that the goal should not be to eliminate it, as the rational-comprehensive model suggests, but to plan in such a way that uncertainty becomes a condition to be taken into account.

No one of whom I am aware, however, has argued that technical knowledge should be abandoned. Rather, the criticism is that it is insufficient. As the U.K. planning theorist Patsy Healey (1992a) has pointed out, professional planning knowledge is not just one thing and it is not simply about how cities, neighborhoods, housing markets, and local economies function. For her, knowing has to occur in five areas: (1) formal governmental procedures, (2) building design, (3) the political–institutional context of planning, (4) the needs and desires of residents of the community, and (5) the likely behavior of influential groups and individuals. In effect, and as Healey implies, planners have to have and should have more than technical knowledge. To expect them to be confined by the science of city building would be to reduce them to narrow-minded experts and, by doing so, suppress the social nature and political impetus of planning. Sound advice depends on more than theories-in-planning. It also requires that planners understand planning's place in the worlds of governments and markets. Planners need theories that explain the functioning of housing markets as well as how elected officials make decisions across multiple objectives and how incentives and regulations compel (or not) conformance to a plan.

The Danish, now U.K., planning theorist Bent Flyvbjerg (2001) agrees. He has written that to truly be an expert, one had to go beyond the scientific understandings, principles, and simplified causal relations commonly associated with technical knowledge. An expert, and here he is expanding a quite common definition, should recognize that planning always occurs in a particular context and that the knowledge associated specifically with that context – not universal, scientific knowledge – is what matters. Absent contextual knowledge, planners will be ineffective. Action cannot happen in the abstract and planning issues are inseparable from the times and places in which they occur. This means that particularities, details often overlooked by mainstream science, are as important as any logic of development. Only through reflection on their experiences in many different planning situations and on the qualities of specific initiatives can planners become true experts. When they do, what they know and how they act becomes experiential rather than formulaic. This demotion of technical knowledge, let alone theory, is also intended to make planners more sensitive to when the collection and analysis of evidence has to cease and action be taken.

The failure to account for context had been previously taken up by the political scientist Edward Banfield (1959) among others. He too accused the rational-comprehensive theorists of ignoring the settings in which planning is done. Banfield pointed to the organizational environment. In public bureaucracies, planners face legal and administrative limits on what can be accomplished. Others (Altshuler 1965; Meyerson and Banfield 1955; Rabinovitz 1969) brought forth local politics as the critical context. Here lie political constraints: elected officials select what problems to address and what solutions to adopt. The application of development controls to a development project, for example, is hardly ever a technical decision. Not only are such controls often ambiguous, but planners also strive for trade-offs among them. These decisions are frequently subjected to influence by elected officials, community groups, developers, and business leaders. The point of this and other criticisms was to suggest that rational, technically inclined planners were casting aside useful knowledge. In response, these critics proposed political theories that embedded planning in interest group politics or political regimes or, for Marxist theorists, the tensions endemic among the state, capitalists, and workers. If planners are going to be influential, they need to navigate planning's political terrain.

Few theorists have been as blunt about this as Bent Flyvbjerg in his widely read *Rationality and Power: Democracy in Practice* (1998). There, he argued that the ineffectiveness of planning is, to a great extent, a consequence of the faulty premise that knowledge is power. When Flyvbjerg probed the difficulties that the planners in Aalborg, Denmark, encountered when they attempted to build a new bus station, re-route traffic, and generally improve the downtown, he found that planning knowledge was of little consequence when confronted by powerful opponents whose influence was immune to what planners had to say. Knowledge was not power. Instead, in his felicitous phrase, "power has a rationality that rationality does not know" (p. 225). The technical knowledge of the planners was easily dismissed by those who had personal connections to local officials and a long history of engagement in local politics. No matter how much high-quality data planners put forth or technical arguments they made, those with power could prevail when they believed that planning would harm their interests. Most importantly, they were able to define reality to suit their interests rather than needing to discover reality through the kinds of systematic investigations that planners are prone to undertake. In effect, power blurs the distinction between rationality and rationalization and this disadvantages planners. For Flyvbjerg, the context of planning is power.[2]

Many of those who argued for contextualizing planning theory also made another criticism: rational-comprehensive models were "ideals" posing as practical procedures. To use a distinction from decision theory, they were normative rather than behavioral. The problem was not with being normative, though, but with offering the rational-comprehensive model as a feasible guide to practice – though see Lichfield (1968). The famous criticism here came from Charles Lindblom (1959), who proposed disjointed incrementalism as an alternative. Drawing on his understanding of how policy was made within public bureaucracies, he pointed out that neither analysts nor bureaucrats strive for optimal solutions but rather, using a British phrase, "muddle through." Full and unlimited knowledge was not the objective but rather knowledge that aided in justifying solutions that were already being considered. The decision process was driven by what worked in the past, that is, by experience. Experience was equally as if not more important than technical knowledge. In addition, analysts and bureaucrats, Lindblom claimed, thought in terms of realistic possibilities. The emphasis was on what was practically feasible not what was theoretically elegant. Being feasible, in another of his useful insights, meant achieving agreement among decision-makers as to what needed to be done. To this extent, a good decision was an acceptable decision: whether it was technically astute was beside the point. A disjointed incremental approach to planning thereby drastically reduced the importance of scientific knowing and technical knowledge. At the same time, it set the planner within a stream of similar decisions made in political and organizational environments where agreement was much more valuable than being scientifically correct. A technically sound decision for which political support was lacking, to use a much-too-common slur, was an academic exercise.

In effect, Lindblom's argument voided any thought of a centralized and top-down approach in which planners alone (supported by elected officials) would have the authority to act. Rather than being neatly organized or amenable to being organized, the policy process was messy. In actuality, and with the exception of authoritarian regimes, numerous actors and their interests engage in a process of mutual adjustment and political compromise and planners have to take their place as just another interest group. Lindblom also implied, similarly to complexity theorists, that the city was not as knowable as planners assumed. The collective outcomes that planners desired would have to be achieved "through the repeated actions of bottom-up decisions" (Batty and Marshall 2009, 570). The city was simply too complex and elusive to be treated otherwise.

For many planning theorists, Lindblom's "muddling through" seemed to be a step too far. Embracing it, they believed, would spell the end to planning. To the rescue came the Israeli-American sociologist Amitai

Etzioni (1967), who proposed a model of planning he called "mixed scanning." Etzioni claimed that the most rational way to proceed in any situation was to recognize the difference between fundamental decisions and incremental decisions. Fundamental decisions set the broad outlines (the strategy) of planning while incremental decisions set the specific actions (the tactics) to be taken. Before a new light rail system is built, a fundamental decision must be made to do so. Only then can the planning of its routes, the selection of its technologies, and the setting of its fare structure occur. Neither a rationalistic approach (borderline utopian in Etzioni's view) nor an incremental approach (borderline conservative) was appropriate. Pivotal for mixed scanning, of course, is knowledge, so much so that Etzioni described this approach as "a particular procedure for collecting information" (p. 389). Strategic decisions entail scanning at a "high level" for broad knowledge of a city or region while tactical decisions require more detailed searches. Rational-comprehensive models seldom make such distinctions and this, for him, was a major flaw. The challenge facing the planner is how to organize knowing so as to identify the various levels of scanning that are needed in a given situation. Etzioni further proposed that these are essentially political distinctions: rationalistic and thus fundamental approaches are often associated with authoritarian regimes and incremental approaches with democratic regimes.[3]

The introduction of politics into planning theory eventually led to a different and more devastating attack on technical knowledge and instrumental rationality. Specifically, the criticism was that the efficacy of experts was dependent not on the quality of their analysis or even the soundness of their advice, but on their ability to be persuasive within a political setting. "In planning practice," as the U.S. planning theorist John Forester (1989, 5) has written, "talk and argument matter." Interpersonal skills, not analysis, are the key to good planning. This does not mean abandoning scientific procedures and technical knowledge. Rather, it means acknowledging that they alone are deficient. Unless planners can shape their advice in ways that appeal to decision-makers, it will go unheeded. To realize this, they need to develop social skills and become familiar with the kinds of concerns that motivate decision-makers to act in one way and not another. For rationality-based theorists, this was theoretically devastating. Since the only knowledge they deemed to be appropriate was technical knowledge, the implication was that (technical) knowledge was not by itself power and, by itself, did not constitute planning. If planners were to have an effect, they would have to be persuasive. And to be persuasive they would have to devalue the efficacy of the kinds of knowledge that they preferred. This did not mean, however, devaluing all knowledge or even all technical knowledge.

I will come back to this repositioning of planning and its relationship to communicative action and collaboration in the chapter on "engaging." For now, one aspect of this turn from analysis requires comment. It concerns misinformation. If planners are to venture outside their offices and become more involved politically and with the residents of the city, then they are likely to encounter various forms of distorted and biased information. Forester (1989, 27–47) pointed to this possibility when he argued that planners have to accept that talk frequently strays from what the German philosopher Jürgen Habermas described as ideal speech. Rather, people speak with partial knowledge filtered through their values, social position, prejudices, and agendas. It is hardly ever the case that people (including planners) speak comprehensively, sincerely, appropriately, and accurately in the ways that ideal speech requires. Moreover, not everyone is a legitimate speaker or to be trusted. Consequently, knowing in social settings is much different from knowing in technical settings where strict rules are widely embraced and policed. The truth is elusive in a much different way. This does not mean that it becomes impossible to act effectively or even usefully. It simply means that talk is never wholly innocent. Planners should not be naïve.

Given this perspective, it would be easy to become cynical. Forester, however, takes a different tack. He argues that planners have an obligation to dispel misinformation and resist distorted communication. This obligation stems from the need to make planning a genuinely democratic process. He goes even further to claim that planners' influence is rooted in their control over information. Information, for him, is a source of power. The implication is that the technical aspects of knowledge and the political aspects of knowledge are inseparable. As Forester (1989, 31) wrote, "one cannot choose between being technical or being political." (He does not make the less defensible claim that knowledge *is* power.) Forester encourages planners to prepare laypeople to participate in the planning process by engaging them in reviewing the facts and by speaking out when those in power distort the issues. In short, planners have to be more than technical experts. And they have to use their access to knowledge for progressive ends.[4]

2.3   Knowledge: dispersed and distributed

Prior to these criticisms, technical knowledge occupied a position of dominance among planning theorists. By excluding non-technical forms of knowing, though, instrumental rationality came to be seen as blocking a more effective planning process as well as a more democratic and inclusionary one. Still, not everyone fully agreed. The Italian planning scholars Luigi Mazza and Marco Bianconi (2014) resisted the relegation of technical understandings to the fringes of planning knowledge. Instead, they asserted that planning knowledge should not be confused with political ideology and called for "a form of knowledge that is substantively autonomous and capable of supporting different and sometimes contrasting political initiatives" (p. 514). Stated this way, Mazza and Bianconi did not oppose the move away from technical knowledge's dominance as much as they called for the restoration of "an adequate and coherent technical language" (p. 525) that does not dissolve planning knowledge in other types of knowledge. Nonetheless, two concerns have to be conceded: first, the need to incorporate more diverse ways of knowing and, second, the need to recognize that the sources of knowledge useful for planning are not confined to experts but distributed across planners and non-planners. A response to both of these concerns has been to bring more residents of the city into the planning process, whether through mechanisms such as public meetings or through collaboration.

I will address participation more fully in the next chapter. For now, I want to consider how the involvement of non-planners (and specifically a city's residents) came to be a way of adding different informational content to the planning process. The twinned idea here is that science should not be privileged and technical knowledge is not the only knowledge of worth. Technical knowledge often ignores what cannot be measured and is weak when it comes to capturing the contextual particularities of a given situation. To technical knowledge has to be added what might be called local knowledge, that is, knowledge about particular places and people's experiences of them.[5] Cities and regions are often highly differentiated with, for instance, retail areas in affluent neighborhoods being distinct from those in low-income ones. Residents live in particular neighborhoods, work in specific areas of the city, spend hours traveling to work on the bus, and frequent nearby parks. They have a detailed understanding of these places that planners lack.

Planners cannot be expected to have local knowledge for every part of the city. Yet, many theorists argue, this is precisely the knowledge that will enable them to develop better plans, write more appropriate regulations, gather support, and be more effective. Consequently, they have to talk with bus riders and neighborhood residents and develop ways in which planners and residents can come together to discuss what is happening, why it is a problem (or an opportunity), and what might be done. In addition, they need to add local knowledge to their calculations and deliberations so that their technical knowledge can be adapted to the context to which it refers.

More than the effectiveness of planning is at stake here. The call to bring local knowledge into planning also has a democratic impulse. Community residents want to be consulted when planners are making decisions that will affect their daily lives, the future of their neighborhood, or the public services available to them. Professor of planning at the University of California: Berkeley Jason Corburn's comment on environmental policy applies to all of planning: "lay people ... are demanding a greater role in researching, describing, and prescribing solutions to ameliorate the local hazards they face" (Corburn 2003, 420).

One way to think about planners and local knowledge is in terms of where knowledge is gathered and assessed. Or, to state it a bit differently and as a question, where does planning happen (i.e., where is it situated?) and how does this influence the knowledge that planners have? The premise is that knowledge is situated. Along these lines, the South African planner Tanya Winkler (2011) has proposed three types of spaces in which planning and activism occur: closed, invited, and claimed. In closed spaces, decision-makers (specifically, governmental officials) deliberate in isolation. When officials want to hear from the public, they create spaces where they can control (more or less) the format of the encounter. These are invited spaces. Claimed spaces are the result of popular mobilizations where protest and debate happen beyond the surveillance of the government. Not only are attendees different in each space, but the interactions among them and the knowledge appropriate to the settings also differ: local knowledge is more prevalent in claimed spaces, technical knowledge in closed spaces.

In Beauregard (2013), I take a parallel approach that focuses on the many places where planning occurs. Planning does not happen solely in the offices of the planning agency. Rather, it is often distributed across different types of places. When planners want to consider the technical considerations of a project, they are most likely to retire to the conference room of the planning office. When they want local knowledge, they leave their offices and go into the community. When the planning director wishes to discuss the politics of the project, he meets with the mayor in her office. Public meetings at a community center allow for people to share their experiences and express their concerns. Focus groups designed to elicit people's desires are held in a classroom of a neighborhood school. In these diverse places, different types of discussions ensue and different kinds of knowledge are considered.

An important illustration of this comes from Donald Schön (1982), who taught for many years at the Massachusetts Institute of Technology (MIT) in the United States. Schön proposed that technical knowledge was not immutable but was negotiated and took different forms in different contexts. When planners work with developers on a specific project, facts and regulations are constantly being interpreted and reinterpreted in light of what is being proposed, the site on which it is to be located, the community that surrounds it, and the future that planners imagine for the city. In the conference room in which they meet, planning knowledge is made and made useful. This knowing-in-practice turns technical knowledge into a local knowledge that enables people to act at specific times and in specific places and allows projects to proceed or not. Schön (1983) claims that these situated deliberations overcome the tendency of experts to attempt to fit the world into pre-existing frameworks. He wrote: "Whenever a professional claims to 'know,' in the sense of the technical expert, he imposes his categories, theories, and techniques on the situation before him. He ignores, explains away, or controls those features of the situation, including the human beings within it, which do not fit" (p. 345). Reality, however, resists and planners are frequently forced to adjust their technical knowledge in light of the concrete possibilities with which they are faced.

Obviously, the type of knowledge that is revealed is related to how it is collected. Technical knowledge can be taken from census documents. Local knowledge has to be gathered by observing first-hand or by interacting with neighborhood residents, park users, or bus riders. The latter might take the form of face-to-face encounters, online surveys, or public meetings. Public meetings are particularly important. They were initially developed to share planning knowledge with citizens, not to collect local knowledge. The aim was to inform citizens of the government's plans for locating new playgrounds, prohibiting development on flood plains, or changing the neighborhood zoning. The premise was that once residents were informed of the reasoning behind these proposed projects, they would be more likely to recognize their rational basis and acquiesce to their implementation. Effectively, knowledge (information) was to be passed from planners to citizens. Once citizens were enlightened, as rational beings they would realize that what the planners were proposing was the best response to the situation. The assumption is that people share the worldview of planners and thus the issue is merely one of accepting the facts.

The local knowledge that the planners collect during these meetings is seldom used to modify plans. Certainly, planners learn from these encounters (Innes and Booher, 2004), although what they most often learn is that people oppose what is happening to their community, are upset about not being consulted, are emotionally attached to their neighborhoods, and are angry over the government's seeming insensitivity to their concerns. Such information is far outside the kinds of knowledge planners are comfortable considering. To this extent, such encounters, ubiquitous within the planning framework of most cities, yield information but not knowledge appropriate to a planning perspective. Anger and resistance seem like problems that fall to politicians to resolve.

Clearly, having planners, as experts, explain to an ostensibly uninformed public what needs to be done, with usable knowledge flowing in only one direction, is unacceptable from a democratic planning perspective. In response, a number of planning theorists have proposed thinking of "knowing" as less an analytical task leading to giving advice than a deliberative and collaborative task leading to agreement on what knowledge is to be considered relevant. This shifts the act of knowing from science to social learning (Friedmann 1987, 181–223).

The issue here is democracy. This has meant making planners' involvement with residents not just more inclusive but deliberative as well. Through talk, planning is explained, local knowledge is gathered, professional knowledge is reconsidered, and plans are modified. And people feel as if their concerns have been acknowledged. From a "knowing" perspective, the approach pivots on communicating honestly, sincerely, and transparently and, as importantly, listening. The planner is encouraged to treat planning as an activity that entails numerous social interactions between planners and developers, elected officials, bureaucrats, and residents. Through these interactions, planners learn about the concerns of others and talk through the different options. Inquiry is always tentative, with whatever knowledge that is gathered subject to collective scrutiny. Planners share their technical knowledge and listen to what others say about it, thereby tempering what they think they know with other perspectives. In short, as Healey (2009, 279) has noted, "facts and values, means and ends, analysis and ethics, problems and solutions are as much discovered in these social contexts as they are performed and a priori."

Many who embrace this approach draw on Habermas's writings on communicative rationality. At the core of Habermas's argument is intersubjective reasoning through which diverse communities share their thoughts through technical, moral, and expressive–aesthetic ways of knowing (Healey 1992b). Those participating in these dialogues make knowledge claims and these claims are validated through public deliberation, not by reference to a predetermined logic or scientific principles. Implicit is that planning is a social learning enterprise that occurs in practical settings. The talk that ensues transforms information into knowledge. Knowledge is not imposed but collectively produced. In this way, and ideally, knowing becomes emancipatory for both planners and non-planners. What non-planners bring to these settings is their experiences and local understandings. The knowing that matters is less the technical calculations that occur in the planners' offices than the knowledge gathered when planners meet with people concerned about what is being planned for them and for the places where they live.

Giving specificity to this social construction of knowledge and understanding is the collaborative planning task of joint fact-finding (Innes and Booher 2010, 160–168). The premise is that what counts as relevant knowledge has to be jointly determined by those involved in and affected by planning initiatives, that is, by stakeholders. Together, the stakeholders decide what needs to be known for the initiative to be successful. Data has to be jointly gathered with the different stakeholders deciding what needs to be collected and what information is relevant. So that stakeholders develop a better understanding of each other's positions and perspectives, role-playing is also encouraged. Through these engagements, stakeholders are also exposed to disagreements among experts, while everyone is brought to an appropriate level of relevant and practical knowledge. This is seen as the only path to an uncoerced consensus. Through negotiations, mediations, forums, teamwork exercises, and other collaborative mechanisms, planning knowledge is created. The resultant knowledge is both technical and non-technical, tailored to the situation, and generative of collective action. In collaborative planning, knowing has become social learning.

A similar approach is known as co-production. Jason Corburn in his book *Street Science* (2005) and numerous articles explores how planners and residents in various environmental controversies interact to produce planning knowledge. He argues that "scientific knowledge and political order are interdependent and evolve jointly" (p. 7). This fact requires planners to work with non-planners to bring scientific knowledge into conformance with a world that is provisional and improvised. In this way, planners access the contextual intelligence that they lack while residents develop an appreciation for the utility of expertise. The categories of "local" and "professional" are thus made to overlap. Expertise is problematized, with experts and laypeople viewed as equal in their contribution to the body of relevant information. Science is not considered truth and knowledge production is combined with democratic engagement.

For these reasons, co-production has to include joint data collection along with collaborative analysis and interpretation. What matters has to be publicly deliberated and negotiated between professionals and non-professionals with the participants allowed to relate anecdotes and tell stories that are treated with the same respect as governmental statistics and survey data. The goal is policy-relevant knowledge on which all can agree. Corburn contrasts co-production with two other forms of knowing: the deficit model and the complementary model. The deficit model retains scientific knowledge as privileged while assuming its independence from power relationships. As importantly, it posits laypeople as having a deficit of scientific knowledge making the task at hand one of educating them. Power relationships are suppressed and the approach embodies an implicit paternalism. In the complementary model, laypeople are brought into the planning process to comment on values. They are made responsible for the normative implications of planning, while scientific knowledge remains (or is seen to remain) disinterested and apolitical. In the co-production model, by contrast, scientific knowledge and those who espouse it are stripped of their dominance and planning knowledge is cast as inherently political. To this extent, such knowledge can only be accessed and made relevant through collective endeavors.[6]

Both joint fact-finding and co-production allow people to speak extemporaneously about their experiences and understandings in a way that is often both personal and emotional. For many theorists, particularly feminist theorists, the roots of this position extend deep into epistemology and begin with the rejection of male-dominated master narratives (Sandercock 1998, 78–83). Plans are no longer viewed as inherently authoritative. Rather, their scientific validity and apolitical objectivity are seen to rest on a crumbling philosophical foundation and a falsely imagined critical distance. Moreover, the world is understood as contingent, fragmented, and non-linear with any knowledge we might have unable to escape its inherent ambiguity. This erases the quality of comprehensiveness so beloved by planners, delegitimizes master plans, and makes the singularity of technical knowledge indefensible. Amid a world of cultural differences and plural subject positions, no one narrative is presumed to be exhaustive. Knowing is not universal but, as feminist planning theorists have argued, part of the bodily experience of women and men, white people and people of color, natives and immigrants, lesbians and homosexuals. Both identity and knowledge are embodied.

For the feminist scholars Leonie Sandercock and Ann Forsyth (1992), language and affect are all-important, thereby shifting from knowledge as content to ways of self-presentation. In order to act together, people communicate through talk, with talk often taking the form of narratives. As Sandercock has written: "Planning is *performed* through story, in a myriad of ways" (2003, 12, emphasis in original). Men and women, however, communicate in different ways. As a simplification, men tend to dominate talk, are more task oriented, and are more comfortable with technical language and less comfortable with ambiguity and emotions. Women – not all of course – tend to defer to men in public settings, are less preemptive when they comment, and are more likely to acknowledge their subjectivity. In addition, they tend to be better listeners. And although one should certainly contest such generalizations, they shape how many feminist planners have approached planning deliberations.

Numerous planning theorists have noted how mainstream, technically based planning falsely separates reasons from emotions and passions from politics. Contrarily, they propose that facts are intertwined with subjectivities, while how we know the world, whether in the laboratory or on the streets, is mediated by who we are in both mind and body. To presume that politics is not a field of passions is to misrepresent it.

People's interests and positions are never solely objective, calculative, and strategic but rather always inflected by their multiple subjectivities. And emotions are not solely a source of knowledge, but also influence how people view the decisions that have to be made (Osborne and Grant-Smith 2015). Emotions can also be detrimental when they lead people to close their minds to what others have to say. They have to be treated critically. What is important is that planners are mindful of the psychological depths of emotions and the impact they have on what people are willing to believe.

The Finnish scholar Heli Saarkoski (2002) has proposed a way to negotiate the subjectivities of planning knowledge. She accepts that bias exists and considers it not as a deviation from some truth and thus to be removed but as ubiquitous and unavoidable. Position and subjectivity, she claims, do not make knowledge "hopelessly subjective" (p. 14) but rather are essential to it. She proposes that planners think in terms of good biases that enable more empirically adequate theories and bad biases that lead to false beliefs. Biases should be considered as empirical evidence to be used as planners deliberate and reason together with others. In short, "experiences, values, and subjective positions are not distorting factors in cognitive inquiry: instead, they are instrumental in truth-tracking" (p. 10).

One way to accommodate this plurality of subject positions, the contingency and ambiguity of knowledge, and the bodily experiences and emotions that are ubiquitous in public deliberations is through storytelling (Sandercock 2003). To quote Sandercock and Forsyth (1992, 51), "The storytelling format [gives] a variety of people the courage to be more involved." The objective is to invite empathy for others and open planners to their own subjectivities. For many of these theorists, storytelling is meant to be cathartic rather than instrumental and less about gathering planning knowledge than acknowledging alternative perspectives.

In effect, planners have to set aside time for listening. Doing so connects planners and non-planners by making the former aware of the "cares, hopes, and fears" (Sandercock 1998, 78) of the latter. Consequently, planners should suppress their preference for linear, coherent, and seemingly factual stories and develop an appreciation for stories that are political, repetitive, often inconsistent, and epistemologically agnostic. The reason to listen is not to gather more and more relevant knowledge; instead, it is to attain a deeper appreciation for what it means to live in a world where one is often the object of social change and not its subject. Stories enable people to constitute their place in their communities and, as these stories circulate, create the publics without which democracy would falter.

Storytelling thus broadens the "knowing" of planning. However, if left in this form, it leaves knowing in the realm of talk and listening; it privileges speech and hearing over other bodily senses. We know the world through talk but also through various texts, and these too need to be acknowledged. Sandercock (1995), in her important article "Voices from the Borderlands," calls for the inclusion not only of told stories but also of prose fiction, poetry, graffiti, film, and paintings. To this we might add community murals, rap music, neighborhood blogs, and performance art. These other ways of knowing are no less meaningful for expressing group solidarities and personal subjectivities. Needed within planning is an epistemology of multiplicity that recognizes the many ways that people express their relationship to others and to place. For Sandercock, doing so recognizes both differences and marginality, thereby acknowledging the injustices that planners are obliged to address.

The multiplicity to which Sandercock and others refer is not simply a matter of plural subjectivities. It entails institutional relations as well and, specifically, transnational relationships of two types. First, there are the global flows of finance, people, commodities, and ideas and their impact on cities and regions (Roy 2011; Yiftachel 2006). Second, there is the development planning that originates in the global North (and West) – the metropole – and is practiced in the global South (and East) – the periphery. The critical premise is one we have already encountered: planning knowledge is sensitive to and shaped by context. As regards a global perspective, planning's ideas and its theory are primarily generated in affluent and powerful countries where they are supported by nation states, transnational corporations, elite universities, well-funded development agencies, and international financial bodies. The questions thus arise as to whether this North-West planning knowledge is sufficiently attentive to and appropriate for global relations as seen from other places and whether European and liberal democratic ways of thinking and acting are applicable in the global South-East.

The challenge for planning knowledge is how to incorporate global ways of knowing while recognizing that knowledge is embodied and situated geographically and while avoiding the universalizing tendencies of planning that would marginalize cultural and other differences. For the American scholar Karen Umemoto (2001), it is not just a matter of knowledge but more basically of knowing. Planners have "to extend their thinking into other epistemological worlds" (p. 17). They have to traverse interpretive frames, confront otherness, respect cultural protocols, and grasp the multiple meanings embedded in language. The South African planning theorist Vanessa Watson (2003) has proposed that the issue is one of conflicting rationalities, that is, "fundamentally different worldviews and different value systems" (p. 396) along with different structures of power and oppression that make Northern planning theories inappropriate for Southern application. The concern here is with falsely claiming that planning knowledge is universal and, ostensibly much like science, relevant across a world of diverse cultures, institutional forms, ethical practices, and socioeconomic conditions (Harrison 2006). More practically, Oren Yiftachel (2006, 214) notes how liberal, North-West ideas "reflect the concerns and intellectual landscapes of these progressive liberal societies" where property values are stable, personal liberties are more or less affirmed, and basic welfare needs are met. The planning task is to recognize the spatial situatedness of knowledge. The theoretical task is to bring a transnational and transcultural perspective to how we think about the planning process.

2.4 Conclusion

In the world of planning theory, knowing has a pivotal role. Without knowledge, planning cannot happen. When people act in its absence, they are doing something else altogether. For theorists, the questions become how knowing should take place, where it should occur, and what mix of knowledge is most appropriate. At the theoretical beginning, technical and professional knowledge (wrapped in instrumental rationality) was all that mattered. Critiqued from numerous directions, it became clear that other types of knowledge – knowledge more contextualized, more political, more experiential, more personal – was also obligatory. The focus turned from systematic research to collaborative inquiry involving joint fact-finding and co-production and from scientific objectivity to subjectivity with the latter creating an opening for emotions and experiences and storytelling. In the process, instrumental rationality was downgraded to secondary status. Planning knowledge was now considered to be embodied, situated spatially, and multiplied along its various epistemological dimensions. Knowing was no longer a simple technical task and no longer disengaged from the other core tasks of planning.

NOTES

1 For theorists with a phenomenological bent (Whittemore 2014), people's knowledge is less important than their experiences.

2 Saarkoski (2002, 12) appropriately reminds us that although "knowledge claims are shaped by power relations," power is not hegemonic over all knowledge.

3 Mixed scanning, of course, echoes the proposal by Perloff that planners should be "generalists with a specialty."

4 Rarely mentioned in the planning theory literature is false consciousness, the Marxist counterpart to misinformation.

5 "Local" here refers to context-specific knowledge in contrast to knowledge deemed to be universal (i.e., applicable anywhere). The implicit contrast with global and cosmopolitan should be obvious.

6 Less dominant in the planning theory literature is how the resultant knowledge is turned into authoritative texts on which planning can be based, but see Lake and Zitcer (2012) on collaborative authorship and Beauregard (1991) on textual matters in planning.

3 Engaging

In *Planning in the Public Domain*, his intellectual history of planning, John Friedmann (1987) noted that embedded in the discipline in its formative years was the expectation that, in a distant future, ideological disputes and political antagonisms would be resolved and pressing public issues would become mere technical problems. The origins of this argument lie in the late 18th century with the French political theorist Henri de Saint-Simon. But the argument also extends into the 20th century with postwar claims of an "end to ideology" and later, with the dismantling of the Soviet Union, the "end of history." No clearer statement of this aspiration exists than August Comte's 19th-century notion of the "administration of things." Taken up by Friedrich Engels and, later, Vladimir Lenin in the early 20th century, the idea was that as political relations were stabilized and class struggle eliminated, a government of persons would be replaced by the administration of conditions, events, facts, and circumstances. By representing the whole of society, not just its factions, socialism would render the state so unnecessary that it would "wither away."

Even though no planning theorist with whom I am familiar embraces such an end to politics, remnants of this strain of thinking nonetheless persist. If one thinks about planning as primarily a matter of making technical decisions regarding how cities and regions function, then the implication is that places can be planned and managed without recourse to either ideology or politics. In fact, ideology and politics are impediments. As we have seen in the previous chapter, however, the general inclination of planning theorists is to reject a planning that is wholly consigned to the administration of things. Its possibility is not even entertained. At minimum, administration involves collaborating with other experts. And, if planning is political (and not merely technical), then it requires levels of involvement beyond other experts: elected officials, local associations, and community groups. "Engaging," the core task to be considered in this chapter, cannot be ignored. Not just a requisite for effective planning, it also contributes to planning's legitimacy and is a source of its political support.

Any discussion of "engaging" begins with planning's institutionalization as a permanent function of local governments in the early 20th century. At that time, its technical side was prominent and the concern was to buffer planning from political influence. By the late 20th century, the focus had shifted and planning was recognized as inherently political. To be legitimate, public planning needed more than the government's imprimatur; it needed to be democratic and open to influence by both elected officials and the city's residents. This meant more than just recognizing local knowledge. It also meant soliciting resident advice and allowing it to shape planning recommendations. If planning is political and is to be democratic as well, then it has to be participatory. Within planning practice, however, engaging entails a much broader set of activities. It is not solely a democratic necessity. Planners also engage when they coordinate their proposals with others, offer advice, and inform decision-makers of their intentions. These forms of engagement exist regardless of what political arrangements are in place. Engaging in this fashion is thus more professional than political. Whether planning is democratic or not, in order to administer things, planners have to share knowledge and engage bureaucrats, elected officials, various experts, and numerous publics.

Before turning our attention to democratic engagement, professional relationships need to be recognized. Coordination, advice-giving, and persuasion are ubiquitous in the daily lives of practicing planners. Despite Friedmann's claim that one of the foundational intellectual bases of planning was organization theory, a perspective primarily concerned with bureaucratic engagement, these relationships are seldom considered in the planning theory literature. After a brief commentary on professional engagements, I will take up the theoretical approaches spawned by the democratic argument for "engaging." This mainly involves communicative practice and collaborative planning (both heavily influenced by pragmatism) but encompasses advocacy planning, citizen participation, and multiculturalism as well. I will also consider theorists who approach planning practice from a radical political position – an insurgent planning – and call for planners to become involved with social movements. I end the chapter by mentioning a small but growing concern with the ways in which planners are entangled with non-human things, thereby tempering the questionable dominance of human-to-human engagement in the planning theory literature.

3.1   Professional engagement

Planners often engage for strictly professional reasons. Within any planning agency, a division of labor exists, with work distributed across various members of the staff and coordination among them being of utmost importance. Planning personnel are also in contact with developers, architects, lawyers, property owners, elected officials, and residents, all of whom have questions and concerns regarding planning regulations. And, because planners do not implement projects but depend on other agencies (e.g., the parks department) to do so, they need to interact with staff there as well. All of these various engagements involve power relations and serve political as well as technical and professional ends. Nonetheless, planners seldom enter into them with democracy as their primary goal.

Of these professional forms of engaging, two of them – coordination and education – have existed since planning's earliest years as a governmental function. As mentioned, Perloff (1957) proposed that planners should be "generalists with a specialty." Associated with knowing and, in part, necessitated by the complexity of cities and regions, this was a comment on engaging as well. The implication is that while local governments require specialized knowledge to deliver public services and regulate private-sector activities, they also require broad knowledge of how these different specialties and their relatively narrow interventions can be coordinated to serve the city as a whole. Local governments (like all complex organizations) need both specialists and generalists. Due to their expansive knowledge of urban and regional development, planners, Perloff believed, are able to perform both roles. Planners can provide a focused expertise as well as coordinate the work of specialized experts so that, for example, elementary schools are provided when new residential subdivisions are ready to be occupied (coordinating education and housing) and land uses adjacent to public reservoirs are properly regulated to avoid pollution run-off (aligning water supply and land use). Planners thereby function as both specialists in land use and generalists in urban and regional development. This means working with personnel from various agencies to ensure mutual compatibility between development initiatives and public service initiatives.[1] Coordination, for Perloff, is one of planning's major tasks and contributions to city building.

Educating the public is another theme that was prominent in the early history of city and regional planning and remains relevant. Its objective was to increase planning's legitimacy and public support. One notable example is the Chicago City Plan of 1909 by the famous architect Daniel Burnham. The City Beautiful plan that he devised was supplemented by the writing of a textbook that explained how cities worked and that noted the necessity of citywide, civic-based planning. The textbook publicized the plan and informed the public and from 1911 to 1924 was distributed to the city's public schools. In a similar vein, public meetings were also initially conceived as educational, that is, as events at which planners would inform residents of what they were proposing and why. And, in a number of cities, planning agencies have set up permanent display spaces to educate and inform the public. Two examples of this are the Helsinki (Finland) City Planning Department's permanent exhibition space (Laituri) in the city center that is opened to the public on a daily basis and the Urban Planning Exhibition Center in Shanghai that houses a scale model of the city.

As regards more interpersonal, professional relations, a small number of theoretical writings consider how planners engage with developers, architects, lawyers, and property owners who are proposing to build on or modify land and/or buildings. The discussion here is not about being democratic but rather about how to mediate between planning regulations and building proposals and thereby coordinate what is being proposed with what has been planned. The central focus for these theorists are the conversations that enable this coordination to occur. Two examples will suffice.

The first case is from Patsy Healey (1992a) and concerns a meeting between a planning officer of a large city in the United Kingdom and an architect regarding the conformance of a proposed building to planning regulations and city council policy. Drawing on a verbatim transcript of the discussion, Healey reflected on the implications for similar planning encounters. She noted how the planner presented and probed for information, controlled the agenda, imagined how the proposal would translate into a built project, and worked with the architect to achieve agreement on how best to present the project to the city council for approval. The focus was on a micro-engagement in which two people negotiate how to make a proposal compliant with planning goals and regulations.

The second example was written by John Forester (1996). His case is an encounter between members of a U.S. planning staff and the developer, architect, and lawyer that involved a proposed apartment building. Reflecting on what was said at the meeting, Forester, as did Healey, commented on aspects of the interaction that have implications for planners' engagement in similar situations. His primary interest was with how planners make practical judgments in the flow of conversation. Unsurprisingly, Forester found that these discussions were more circuitous than linear, with the planners commenting, proposing, asking for clarification, circling back to earlier issues, and exploring possibilities. The project's advocates behaved similarly with both groups, searching for a way to move the project forward, respect planning regulations, acknowledge the developer's financial and architectural goals, and benefit the city. The engagement was rational and emotional as well as technical and political. As Forester (1996, 258) wrote, planning necessitates "real argumentative work" with people who have the expertise and resources to achieve what planners have envisioned. This is not about engaging to be democratic but rather about engaging to be effective as a planning professional.

Donald Schön (1982) thought about this form of engagement in terms of interpersonal theories of action. He observed that in these situations planners favored an approach that defends their status as experts and treats those with whom they are engaging as petitioners and, at times, adversaries. He called this Model I. In Model I, the planner strives to maintain unilateral control. Her intent is to achieve the task as she has defined it, withhold valuable information, protect her status as the planner, avoid negative feelings, block any testing of her assumptions, and strive to remain wholly rational. The goal is not just to control the discussion but to win (i.e., to make the developer conform to the regulations as the planner interprets them). Planners seek "to master the situation while keeping their own thoughts and feelings mysterious" (p. 360). This causes the non-planner to take a similar approach, with both the planner and the non-planner acting strategically in order to achieve their objectives in what each conceives to be a win–lose situation. Such a deliberative style, Schön argued, leads to suboptimal results. Relevant knowledge is left unexamined and useful compromises remain unspoken. Additionally, the Model I planner casts aside numerous opportunities to reflect on how she and the city government think about planning and development; that is, they fail to do more than proceed in a narrow-minded, functionally rational fashion.

As an alternative, Schön proposed what he labeled a Model II approach to "knowing-in-practice." In Model II the planner and the non-planner engage each other as if a win–win outcome is possible. They seek valid information and receive it in return. The tone of the meeting is one of free and informed choice such that prior experiences, capacities, and limits are jointly recognized. Talk is transparent, assumptions are openly considered, and dilemmas are presented for discussion. Together, the participants search for a compromise that, because it is collaboratively arrived at rather than dictated by the planner, can be considered satisfactory. The end result is a decision that each party supports. Moreover, the planner and her collaborator now have a better understanding of how to think about the city's development and of the strengths and weaknesses of planning regulations. At the end of their encounter, each feels that the meeting has been productive. Performing effectively and, in the case of Model II, being respectful of others were the objectives.

3.2   Democratic intentions: practical approaches

Engaging is also discussed by planning theorists as part of the belief that planning should be democratic. As Healey (1992b, 145) has written, "The modern idea of planning ... centres on the challenge of finding ways in which citizens, through acting together, can manage their collective concerns." This democratic impulse is unsurprising given that almost all planning theory is written by scholars living in liberal, democratic societies. And while these societies have a few scholars leery of "big" government and who argue that planning should adhere more closely to market principles or be dispensed with altogether, the great plurality of theorists believe in a democratic planning. In a democracy, non-planners should have opportunities to influence planners and, by doing so, make planning publicly accountable. Democratic engagement also dampens the tyranny of experts and shields planning from an oligarchic politics that favors narrow interests over those of the larger public and the city. In the broadest terms, a planning process open to democratic participation derives legitimacy from the public and this reinforces the legitimacy planning receives from being a governmental function.

One of the earliest manifestations of the perceived need for democratic planning occurred when planning became part of the institutional structure of local governments in the early 20th century (Thorpe 2017). Within many countries, the planning function was positioned such that the planning staff reports to elected officials (e.g., a chief executive or city council) through an intermediary. Within the United States, this intermediary is a planning commission composed of community residents appointed by elected officials, which (by law) has to open its meetings to the public (Innes and Booher 2004, 423–424). In the United Kingdom, the intermediary is a local planning authority made up of members of the city council. And in Helsinki, Finland, the planning staff is overseen by a City Planning Board elected by the political parties in the City Council. Members of the Board can be, but do not have to be, from the Council. These intermediaries provide a buffer between planners and elected officials acting politically. And, in the U.S. and Finnish case, they allow residents to be involved in directing and approving (or not) planning proposals, regulations, and plans. Of course, and in almost all instances, those selected for these intermediary bodies tend to be individuals with an interest in developmental issues – for example, large property owners, bankers, and directors of environmental groups. Participation is thus confined to people with a general stake in planning issues. The alternatives are to dispense with an intermediate entity and have the planning staff report directly to the governing body or allow the planners to rule independently. The former might well exist, but I suspect the latter does not.

A second and quite common way of engaging democratically is via public meetings and community forums (Innes and Booher 2004). The major purpose of public meetings is to allow residents of a community to review and comment on plans and proposals being considered by the local government. The planners explain what they are doing as regards a specific issue, such as restricting development in a flood-prone area, and the public is allowed to voice their concerns. The planners' primary goal is to convey information. This is a constrained engagement: planners seldom respond to statements made by residents and are mainly there to listen. From the government's perspective, these meetings are not meant to be deliberative. From the planners' perspective they are not meant to be opportunities to systematically gather local knowledge. To this extent, public meetings function as managerial techniques and not democratic engagements, with the maintenance of professional control paramount (Thorpe 2017). Residents, however, want their concerns to be acknowledged. They want to discuss what should be done and why. When this does not happen, and when the issue is contentious (e.g., locating a homeless facility in the neighborhood), the public is often antagonized. This leads to the meeting becoming adversarial. In short, a public meeting is a variant of Schön's Model I approach to action: planners maintain control over the planning process even though they risk losing control of the meeting. A better way to describe public meetings is not as a constriction of engagement, but as co-presence without engagement. As one critic (Thorpe 2017, 577) has commented, such public meetings are essentially "concessions made by the state to create a discrete space for public involvement" and not an ongoing part of the planning process.

Public meetings are just one, albeit quite common, mechanism in the larger project of ensuring democratic citizen participation (Day 1997). The overarching concern of participation is engaging ordinary residents, whether individuals or organized groups, in ways that enable them to influence what planners recommend to the local government. (Elected officials and agency heads have other ways to participate.) Such participation extends beyond the mandate of the city's planning agency. In a number of countries, and since about the mid-20th century, governments have funded programs (e.g., in community development) that require citizens to be consulted if funding is to be made available. This often means establishing program advisory boards composed of residents. The democratic benefits include the gathering of local knowledge, greater governmental accountability, the overcoming of public apathy, and (hopefully) a planning process seen as more legitimate by the public: "Participation is a central element in a theory of planning in which the planner's function is to analyze and synthesize the goals and values of the community" (Reynolds 1969, 132).

Citizen participation, though, is not without its problems. One nagging issue is representativeness, that is, who actually participates. Usually it is the politically active and those who have the time to do so, leaving out a good portion of the population. Then there is the problem of how planners can incorporate into their recommendations the contrasting views of diverse publics. Most bothersome for practicing planners and local governments is how much influence to give to residents. The last is the focal point of a famous article by Sherry Arnstein (1969) titled "A Ladder of Citizen Participation."[2]

Arnstein developed a typology of participation based on her involvement with three federally funded U.S. governmental programs concerned with community development. Her article (and argument) has two premises: that planning should be responsive to the will of the people and that citizen participation should empower the poor and the powerless. On this basis, she constructed an eight-step ladder of citizen participation ranging from manipulation and tokenism at the bottom to citizen power at the top. On the lowest two rungs are, first, manipulation, in which planners control a meeting and deflect any input from residents and, second, therapy, in which the goal of public engagement is simply to allow residents to complain. The next three steps involve tokenism. Put simply, these steps are informing, consultation, and placation. On the placation rung, planners commiserate with residents but do nothing to alleviate their anxieties. The top three steps, and the steps which Arnstein prefers, are partnership, delegated power, and citizen control. From step 6 to step 8, citizens become more autonomous regarding the influence that they can wield, to the point where they become the actual decision-makers. At this level, this might mean, as Karen Umemoto (2001) has pointed out, allowing citizens to design and facilitate the planning process including controlling the agenda, where meetings occur, and who is invited to speak.[3]

Advocacy planning provides residents with more influence than they would otherwise have but only partly remedies problems of representativeness. Having planners become advisors to citizen groups and moving planning itself closer to and under the influence of residents, makes planning more inclusive but only partially fulfills the democratic impulse. Advocacy planners are encouraged to work with groups with whom they share common interests and a political orientation. Yet, in their advocate role, they remain experts and advice-givers. The expert/non-expert divide is left intact. Admittedly, the planning process is brought to the residents rather than vice versa, but residents are not "equals" (as regards technical knowledge) and, to this extent, are disempowered from Arnstein's point of view. In addition, not all residents, for various reasons, are going to participate in meetings with the advocacy planners. And they are still clients of the planning process and have the restrictions attendant to that role. An advocacy relationship, moreover, can easily slip into one of unilateral control by the planners – Model I behavior in Schön's terms.[4] Whether or not advocacy planners working for a non-governmental group or from within the government view themselves as advocates for those less fortunate (Krumholz 1982), the relationship is less one of citizen power and more one of consultation. Consequently, it is low on Arnstein's ladder. Citizen participation at its highest rungs would turn residents into planners.

The notion drawn from advocacy planning that planners should work only for those with whom they share political positions has another political dimension, one involving social movements (Beard 2003; Friedmann 1987, 225–308). Particularly within the just-city and right-to-the-city literatures, a belief exists that a just planning is only possible when social movements bring public pressure on insensitive governments and exploitative corporations to act in just ways. Significant social change happens through opposition and resistance. Social justice cannot be found in a governmental planning that is, at best, reformist. More basic change is needed and this is unlikely if planners work within the government or advocate for relatively isolated groups. Planners must, instead, become involved in anti-globalization movements, anti-racist coalitions, citywide anti-gentrification initiatives, and corporate boycotts. They must develop an insurgent planning that is "counter-hegemonic, transgressive, and imaginative" (Miraftab 2009, 32). The hope for justice resides in the success of social movements and the hope for social movements resides in building coalitions.

How planners engage within these movements, beyond declaring their solidarity, is not well articulated. Contributing time, money, expertise, and one's body (e.g., at protest marches) is implied, but this hardly distinguishes planners from any other participant. I suspect that the actual tasks that radical planners would perform are not that much different than what is expected of an advocacy planner, that is, providing technical research and advice. Again, this maintains the expert–client relationship. Forming networks of opposition groups who can share resources and ideas, moreover, is not a skill unique to planners and certainly not their strength as the profession has been conceived. As advocacy planners discovered, the groups in need of planning have many other and more important needs, and what planners can do best is whatever needs to be done. To this extent, critical for theorists making this argument is that planners find ways to engage politically in a world that is persistently unjust and deeply unequal.

Adding to the issues of representation and influence that participation poses to democratic planning are two others that are even more daunting. One is the ambivalence that planners have toward participation (Monno and Khakee 2012). Planners want to involve residents in the planning process in a meaningful way, but they are also protective of their prerogatives as experts and professionals. To maneuver participation to the top of Arnstein's ladder where residents become decision-makers, threatens their role in the government. Equally bothersome and problematic is the tendency to reify the interests and identities of "the people." Publics are constructed in relation to the planning issue. Moreover, planners frequently assume these publics to be not just homogeneous in their interests but progressive in their values. For most critical theorists, as the U.K. scholar Yasminah Beebeejaun (2006, 15) has observed, participation substitutes influence over development disputes for engagement with the very processes of "embedded racial and social inequalities" faced by low-income and marginalized residents.

3.3 Democratic intentions: theoretical approaches

A more theoretical approach to engaging comes from theorists whose interests revolve around communicative practice, collaboration, and pragmatism. These are not distinct perspectives but rather variations on a common commitment to building advice from below. With roots in resident participation, they also represent a shift away from both the rational-comprehensive model (with its belief that knowledge is discovered and not constructed) and the Marxist political economy that emerged during the 1970s in response to the period's social and economic turmoil. A general democratic impulse of the time encouraged the greater involvement of residents and, within academia, led to the questioning of the anti-democratic tendencies of a planning process that privileged technical analysis and instrumental rationality – and thus experts – over local knowledge and ordinary residents. Marxist-based planning theory also came under attack for its obsession with class struggle and seeming indifference to democratic engagement. Many theorists recognized that for planning to be effective, planners would have to more politically engaged but not in an oppositional fashion. Planners would have to persuade others of the usefulness of their recommendations while developing plans and proposals in tandem with non-planners. Analytical sophistication alone, these theorists acknowledged, was rarely politically convincing. For them, communication became the key to effective planning. To achieve their objectives, planners would have to be better at talking and listening to others. As John Forester (1989, 23) wrote, "nothing is done until it is first said."

Many of these theorists were heavily influenced by the work of Habermas, particularly his writings on communicative rationality and the relationship of the state to the public sphere (Huxley 2000). Habermas believed that consensus could be achieved through speech acts; that is, that talking together was an essential prelude to any commitment to collective action. He also postulated, less optimistically, that scientific rationalism was too easily subverted and redirected to non-progressive, non-liberal ends. Communicative rationality necessitated the replacement of the self-conscious, autonomous subject with a subject engaged in intersubjective communication. The mutual understanding that would result would be laced through with factual, emotional, moral, and aesthetic concerns but also provide an opportunity to correct disinformation. To this extent, Habermas jettisoned both instrumental rationality associated with science and strategic rationality associated with power-based politics. Non-coercive deliberation and intersubjective knowledge would be the basis for transforming the public sphere and bringing about a liberal society in which people would find acceptable ways to act together to realize shared interests. To make this happen, people would have to strive, as much as possible, to achieve ideal speech, that is, speech that is comprehensible, sincere, legitimate, and accurate. In effect, communicative rationality required a deliberative democracy for its legitimacy. This was the setting for "ideal" communication (Sager 2013).

As Forester (1989, 27–47) interpreted Habermas, the role of the planner is to ensure that planning deliberations are honest and transparent as well as inclusive. More specifically, planners are to reveal the ways in which power distorts information (and ideal speech) for its own gains. The communicative planner's goal is to realize a critical, self-reflective, and emancipatory practice.

In communicative practice theory, then, the planner gives as much (if not more) attention to interacting with others as to technical problems. When discussing a proposal from a developer or property owner, when meeting with a neighborhood group, or when presenting in front of the planning authority, the planner strives to speak truthfully and transparently, listen to and learn from others, share (rather than hide) concerns and knowledge, be respectful, and recognize and accept that people are often passionate about the planning issues that directly affect them and that their emotions are as important as their objective interests. In these encounters, planners are still instrumental, for one of their objectives is to shape the attention of participants to enable the discovery of mutually agreeable solutions to common concerns. The end point of communicative practice, though, is a consensus in which people arrive at shared understandings in a non-coercive manner. Here also lies planning's legitimacy. Interpersonal relations occurring in social settings are the key to planning's effectiveness.

The approach can also be extended beyond the ideal speech setting to the realm of discourse, that is, perspectives that privilege certain language and ideas and, consequently, encourage certain actions over others. In this variation, interpersonal relations are replaced by already-present and shared understandings embodied in how people talk about the world. Drawing on his sense of planning as linking knowledge to action, Friedmann (1989) proposed that planning discourse is "nourished" by three streams of discourse: a moral discourse concerned with ethical choice, a technical discourse, and a utopian discourse that imagines alternative visions of the "good life." The planner's task is to engage in these discourses with others in order to engender a political dynamic that leads to collective action. What distinguishes this discursive approach from communitive practice is the belief that communication occurs within pre-existing rhetorical structures.

Rather than looking inward to planning talk as Friedmann did, James Throgmorton (1996), another American planning theorist, turned outward to the even larger narratives in which planners find themselves. These narratives are crafted stories that establish the discursive context in which planning occurs. For example, in the United States, the dominant urban narrative focuses on economic growth, privileges a creative class of people, and celebrates the importance of quality public spaces for attracting an educated middle class. For planners to be effective, Throgmorton (2000) observed, they have to be able to make persuasive arguments within these narratives while introducing counter-narratives that elevate planning concerns beyond mundane and conservative interests. He simultaneously recognized the importance of contextualizing discourses and maintained that the task of the planner was to be persuasive in the face of existing, even if contested, worldviews. In his felicitous phrase, planners have to be a "skilled voice in the flow of persuasive argumentation" (2000, 367).[5]

Patsy Healey developed communicative practice around another form of engagement – collaboration (Healey 2006; 1992b). For her, planning is not simply a matter of communicating in ways that facilitate understanding. Rather, she broadened her perspective to encompass institutional relations that constrain how people collectively construct their worlds – that is, achieve agency. Her interest is in how social interactions produce shared understandings and mutual trust that then enable people to overcome the differences that divide them. Planning tasks are defined during deliberative engagement not prior to it. Consequently, planning becomes a form of governance grounded in the development of strategies that craft relational networks in specific places. The goal of planning is to build institutional (or relational) capacity so that people can find ways to live together harmoniously and share power, a position that Sherry Arnstein would enthusiastically support. Of note, and in common with procedural approaches to planning, she expects planning to be inclusive of all stakeholders and, despite the conflict that this might engender, to explore ways of channeling that conflict to common ends. The implication is that resolutions are possible: as she optimistically writes (Healey 2006, 243), "an interest [exists] among stakeholders in the design of institutional processes which will facilitate collaboration, mutual learning and consensus-building."

The role of the planner in this framework is to develop strategic collaborations. In fact, Healey (2006, 248) sees strategy-making as "the heartland of planning culture." Importantly, she does not confine strategy-making to consensus-building. Healey has a longer time frame in mind. She wants these collaborations to build institutional capacity within and across relational networks. Planners can do this by engaging in a communicative practice that attends to practical consciousness and local knowledge, encourages reflection on the part of participants, builds relationships, and formulates new ways of thinking that enable collective action to be taken despite cultural and political differences among stakeholders. Planning thus becomes an intersubjective process in which the planner is responsible for an inclusive and collaborative dialogue that focuses on people's place-based interests. This form of engaging is then situated within a communicative practice that values openness, listening, mutual learning, respect, and emotional awareness, with all this occurring through talk.

Judith Innes and David Booher (2010; 2004; 1999) opted for a different path to collaborative planning, though one still anchored in the interactive and intersubjective precepts of communicative practice. Innes (a U.S.-based professor emeritus of planning) and Booher (a U.S. planning consultant) developed their approach by engaging in collaborative planning in the Bay Area of San Francisco (U.S.A.), where they brought together stakeholders around environmental issues. Collaboration, they argue, is most necessary in situations where difficult and contentious issues need to be resolved, where stalemate is possible and detrimental, and where stakeholders can block an issue's resolution. In these situations, planners need to facilitate communicative interaction.

To do so, they must overcome the perception that because they are governmental employees, they have an agenda that precludes them from serving as a neutral party.

Having brought representatives of diverse interests into a room, facilitators engage with them to develop consensus around an issue that everyone wants resolved. These meetings often begin with joint fact-finding, in which the participants work together to develop knowledge of the issue. Guided by the facilitator–planner, the participants come to agreement on what facts matter and what they mean. Only then do they formulate recommendations. To arrive at this end point of the collaboration, they engage in role-playing, storytelling, and speculative thinking about what is possible and what might be the consequences. One of the objectives is to encourage stakeholders to view the situation from the perspective of others. As Innes and Booher (2010, 113) have written, stakeholders should "stand up for their own interests without denying others the same opportunity." Dialogue is open, control is distributed, everyone is treated equally, and learning is mutual. Consensus on what to do brings the collaboration to an end, at least for the moment, and leaves behind civic capacity and the trust that will enable people to collaborate when their interests once again intersect. The planner's role is to provide a generative rather than directive leadership.

The casting of the planner as a facilitator of collaboration goes well beyond the planner as a technical expert or the planner as an interested party in discussions with property owners, developers, and elected officials. In collaborative planning, the social setting is much larger and the interests more diverse. Additionally, the planner no longer brings an agenda to the meeting, but allows the agenda and the final outcome to be determined by the participants. Innes and Booher believe that an agreed-upon resolution has to emerge from stakeholder interactions. The implication is that the planner's expertise is unimportant or, maybe better said, less important than the knowledge that emerges from collaboration. Knowledge, which Friedmann and many others have viewed as a defining element of planning and as controlled to a greater or lesser degree by the planner, now has been distributed across stakeholders. Planners are no more nor no less influential than other participants.

On this point, John Forester (2009), in his later writings, has reinvented the planner as a negotiator and mediator amid public conflicts rather than as an expert shaper of attention and advice. In such contentious situations as inter-municipal disputes and the writing of regulations for visitor use of national parks, planners take the role of directive leaders who work with contending parties to enable them to resolve their differences. They either become directly involved as negotiators or guide the interaction as mediators. In his book *Dealing with Differences: Dramas of Mediating Public Disputes* (2009), Forester presents a series of case studies in which people trained in these roles engage with diverse stakeholders to resolve contentious disputes. His concern is mainly with negotiation-based, collaborative processes (Shmueli, Kaufman, and Ozawa 2008) in which the "planner" takes an active role in defining interests and positions, guiding the ways that stakeholders engage with each other, and using information strategically to uncover a set of mutual gains that allow the issue to be resolved. In this form of engagement, the planner is more than a facilitator and more than a neutral participant. His responsibility is to find ways to achieve resolution, not simply to create the conditions from which a resolution might emerge as with collaborative planning.

Each of these collaborative approaches involves the planner in a slightly different role, but all of them recognize that collaboration almost always involves people from diverse cultural backgrounds. The objective then becomes how to respect cultural identities without allowing identity to be a distinction that blocks consensus. Despite the importance given to cultural sensitivity, however, communicative practice and collaborative planning theorists have little specific to say about how the planner might actually engage with people culturally different than themselves. The planner is encouraged to be respectful and, of course, to listen and be tolerant, regardless of who is speaking, but this is quite general guidance. Feminist theorists and multiculturalists are slightly more forthcoming about how cultural differences are to be handled. Of particular note is the exhortation to listen carefully and respectfully to the stories told by cultural others. In fact, planners should encourage such stories (Sandercock 1998, 57–58). No planner can experience the world as another person does, but he can attempt to do so. This is not just a matter of recognizing that people from different backgrounds might have different interests. Rather, it entails emotional work in which the planner strives for an empathic connection.

The various qualities of engaging expressed in communicative practice and collaborative planning have in common the arguments put forth by American pragmatic philosophers. One of pragmatism's attractions for planning theorists is its anti-foundationalism (Healey 2009; Hoch 1984b). Pragmatism rejects the notion that there are absolute truths waiting to be discovered and from which practical arguments can be extracted. Neither absolutes nor certainty are available to us, they claim, and, consequently, control is elusive. Knowledge is fallible and demands constant examination, modification, and critique. This can only come about through social inquiry in which people draw on their experiences to reflect on the value of knowledge. Together, they deliberate around mutual interests – responding to problems – in the hopes of discovering appropriate resolutions. By deliberating as equals, sharing prior experiences, and experimenting with a variety of different possibilities, they can then move toward an action on which they can agree.

The test for knowledge lies in its practical consequences, not its truthfulness. If knowledge produces an action whose consequences are those which were expected and predicted, then it is useful knowledge. If it does not, then social learning occurs and another round of deliberations begins. Truth is beside the point. What matters for action is not truth but warranted assertability; that is, an understanding that holds up to critique and survives being tested in real-world situations. Or, to write it differently, what matters is experimentation: taking action and learning from the experience of doing so.

What further attracts many planning theorists to pragmatism is that its inquiry is meant to be democratic and moral. The pragmatists, particularly its leading proponent, the philosopher John Dewey, believed that deliberations should be public – that is, open to all people who share a concern and wish to explore its resolution – and that within these deliberations, all experiences are equally valued. No experts exist whose knowledge is expected to be judged as more valuable than the knowledge of non-experts. Technical knowledge is different not superior. In addition, inquiry is morally based. People participate using the full range of their humanity. Material interests, moral concerns, and aesthetic judgments are all acceptable, for pragmatists recognize that public decisions are hardly ever solely technical. Out of this comes a collective decision that is designed to be not merely effective (i.e., producing the intended consequences) but morally appropriate as well. In this sense, pragmatism (or critical pragmatism in John Forester's formulation) brings together the procedural and the substantive: "*pragmatic* enough to relate to planners' real problems of getting something done, and *critical* enough to worry about the quality of *what* in the world gets done and, of course, *for whom* it gets done" (Forester 1999, 176, emphasis in original). For the American planning theorist Charles Hoch (1984a), one of the most attractive qualities of pragmatism is that it allows planners to "be right" and to "do good." Yet, pragmatists are willing to allow the substantive outcomes to emerge from public deliberations and thus seem to be agnostic as regards what should be done, a contentious position within planning theory.[6]

Pragmatism provides one of the major intellectual pillars on which communicative practice and collaborative planning rest. Important to all these theories are practical judgments and their grounding in experimentation, the human capacity for social learning, and discovery "in the flow of life lived in association with others" (Healey 2009, 287). The planner's task is simple: engage with, talk to, and listen to others. Pushed to the side are planners' technical skills, instrumental knowledge, and expert status. What matters is what a democratic public wants done.

3.4   Engaging with things

All of these forms of engaging center on how planners relate to other people. A small group of theorists, however, claim that in order to plan, humans must engage with non-human things as well, and that these non-human things are not simply epiphenomenal (Beauregard 2015; Beauregard 2012b; Lieto and Beauregard 2013; Rydin 2014). Planners plan with "things"; that is, they employ mapping software, computers, smartphones, legal documents, conference room tables, video projectors, and automobiles. Things – playgrounds, highway connections, retention ponds, "green" buildings, and affordable housing – are also the objects of planning.

To the extent that it is concerned with guiding the development and improving the quality of the city's built environment, planning is deeply engaged with the material world. Material conditions affect how planning is done and what can be done. The capacity of an existing landfill site will influence planning for future waste-disposal sites as the city's population grows, the elevation of a seaside shoreline will affect the attention planners give to sea-level rise and climate change, and the amount of air pollution from vehicles will influence the calculations of transportation planners. In her discussion of carbon-emission regulation in London, the U.K. planning scholar Yvonne Rydin (2012) acknowledged the importance of the physical design of buildings, the materials used in their construction, and the energy-efficiency of heating and ventilating systems. Three Finnish planning scholars (Leino, Karppi, and Jokinen 2017) have described how plans to develop a mixed-use area around a large retention pond used by a waste treatment facility attracted bird watchers and other nature-lovers who became concerned about the threat to the habitat posed by residential and commercial development. When planners joined with community groups, elected officials, and developers to discuss how development should proceed, joining them in the room were things of nature. The result was "a complex [planning] process involving artefacts [the water treatment facility], humans and birds" (p. 145).

Planners, then, do not act alone or solely with other people, but almost always with an object that facilitates and constrains their actions. If the thing fails to perform, if the software is faulty for example, the planner's task will be derailed. To treat objects as simply passive and subject wholly to human control is to misread the non-human world, a world in which traffic signals malfunction, rodents nest in bus shelters, retaining walls collapse, and geese invade a public park. Planning action is distributed across humans and their organizations as well as humans and non-humans. To this extent, the intentionality which defines planning is only one form of action. Non-human actors frequently lack intentionality, but they do not lack agency. From this socio-material perspective, an actor – the technical term often used is actant – is anything, human or not, that causes another thing to respond. This approach thus brings into planning such entities as berms and written documents that are not often considered theoretically or even practically important. The equivalence of humans and non-humans dictated by this specific notion of agency produces a democracy of things. In effect, a socio-material approach substitutes a realist ontology for an anti-realist ontology (Harrison 2014). Planners engage – collaborate – with non-human others and this simply cannot be avoided.

Of course, engaging with non-human things is not the same as engaging with humans. Among humans, talk is important, as communicative practice theory and collaborative planning theory attest. In addition, humans share a common language as well as norms and thus have a basic understanding of how to engage with each other. Emotions and physical gestures can be read and responded to appropriately. (Of course, this is less the case when people speak different languages and come from different cultures.) Communication between humans and non-humans is a bit different. Talk is no longer as central. Rather, planners interact in other ways. They manipulate objects, for example, by arranging the chairs around a conference table, bringing a projector into a meeting, or giving commands to a software program. Within their plans, they delegate responsibilities to non-human things – for example, when designing a small plaza to collect storm-water run-off from adjacent residential areas or assigning to the minutes of meetings the responsibility of remembering what decisions were made. And even though these non-human things cannot respond by verbally raising objections and offering a different perspective on what is to be done, they do respond. The software program creates a new map which causes the planner to reconsider how to analyze the data or the plaza fails to absorb all the storm water and has to be augmented or redesigned. Engagement occurs and it is not just one-sided with planners acting and non-human things simply obeying their orders.

From a socio-material perspective, engagement often takes the form of a network. That is, planners are encouraged to see themselves "drawn into associations" (Rydin 2014, 591) across which action is distributed. These associations are essentially assemblages of humans and non-humans that together enable a project to be accomplished. Rather than viewed as intervening in a world outside, planners are positioned as already moving within assemblages in which they had previously enrolled or across different assemblages as they pursue collaborations. They join with others to act. Extensive control over, say, preservation of a wetlands is not something that planners have or to which they should aspire. Rather, control emerges from stabilized relations (assemblages) of which planners are only one set of actors.

A social housing assemblage might consist of planners, developers, elected officials, advocacy groups, architects, local residents, sites, construction equipment, building materials, financing mechanisms, development permissions, soils, and scheduling technologies, all of which are necessary for building affordable homes in the city. What will enable this goal to be reached is the ability of the assemblage to remain stable. Each of these actors has something to contribute, and if one or the other withdraws, the assemblage has to be re-stabilized for it to continue its activities. The question then arises as to what role planners play in these assemblages: how do they engage in this distributed action? No simple answer exists. Planners can share their expertise, they can engage in discussions of alternative perspectives and actions (deploying communicative practice), and they can collaborate. As consequential is that they recognize that they must engage not just with other humans but with non-human things, respecting the fact that these non-human things are themselves active agents. In the words of Yvonne Rydin (2012, 27): "The dance of planning practice is thus about working with actants (social and material) in a variety of small ways, using intermediaries to bring actants into relationships with each other so that traceable associations and resultant action can be generated but in the knowledge that many other associations are at work."

3.5 Conclusion

For many planning theorists, "engaging" is the key to planning, not knowledge. Planning consists of much, much more than the technical administration of things. When the emphasis is shifted in this way, and these theorists begin to think about how knowledge is developed and how it enables planning to be effective and democratic, "engaging" rises above "knowing" as the main activity of practice. Here is where we find the pragmatists, the collaborative planning theorists, and communicative practice. This seems obvious: planners cannot plan unless they engage with others. Yet, planning also includes forms of engagement – professional engagements – that are not pragmatic in this philosophical sense and are not designed specifically to make planning more democratic. Once one understands planning as distributed action, as the socio-materialists encourage us to do, then engagement broadens beyond simply giving advice to elected officials or standing before a packed auditorium to explain why, for example, the boundaries of the city's wetlands have been redrawn. Emerging out of this shift from knowledge and analysis to inquiry and collaboration is a clearer understanding of the moral dilemmas and political aspects of planning and of the difficulty that planners have in prescribing what should be done. This is the topic of the next chapter.

NOTES

1 Citywide coordination and its politics are mostly absent from the planning theory literature, but see Beckman (1964), Benveniste (1977), Krumholz (1982), and Rabinovitz (1969).

2 This is one of the most widely cited and reprinted articles in the field. Arnstein was, during her career, a special assistant and advisor to the U.S. federal government, a policy analyst, and the executive director of a non-profit organization. She was never an academic.

3 Given the current political debate around illegal immigration in many countries, particularly the

United States, the use of "citizen" suggests confining participation only to legal residents. This would be rejected by most planning theorists.

4 For an attempt to avoid this trap, see the experience of Planact, a foundation-funded advocacy group in South Africa, during the late apartheid years (Beauregard 1995).

5 The turn to discourse was part of a postmodern and feminist turn in planning theory. On this point, see Beauregard (1991).

6 This is one of the reasons procedural approaches are criticized by theorists with strong political leanings.

4   Prescribing

In one ideal world, planners would engage solely in the administration of things. All the problems posed to them would be technical problems, stripped of political venality. Such a fate is not within their reach. Not only is it unrealistic, but it is morally problematic as well. The planner's purpose is to convey a particular understanding of how the city is changing and recommend what should be done in response. Doing so requires going beyond the data, beyond the facts of the matter. It requires having a sense of what people value and how they want to live together. It requires being in the world rather than outside looking in. And although giving advice in and of itself makes planning inherently normative, it is only one of the reasons for the artificiality of any claim to being above the fray.

Of even greater consequence for the normative nature of planning is the inability of planners to disconnect themselves from the webs of obligations in which all of us are ensnared. A planner can certainly ignore his moral and political responsibilities; he cannot, though, wholly escape them. For the political philosopher Hannah Arendt, to be in the world was to act in the world; action is what makes people human. And the action that matters is that which occurs when we come together to find ways to coexist absent animosity, impoverishment, and intolerance. The essence of human existence, for Arendt, was deeply rooted in a politics in which people publicly discuss their thoughts and experiences, test their understandings, and, out of this, form publics. For her, politics is a field of words and persuasion, not of force and violence. To be human we have to take up this political responsibility. The implications for planners are clear. To borrow a phrase from the mid-20th-century political writer George Orwell, planners can choose to be "inside the whale," that is, they can choose to be passive and distant and irresponsible, or they can acknowledge their humanity and be engaged. This responsibility to recognize the worldliness of planning establishes the values and relationships on which all planning action is based.

Clearly, I am stretching the task of "prescribing" well beyond making statements about what should be done. For me, prescribing encompasses the ethical and moral responsibilities of planners as well as their ideological beliefs. It reaches to the political core of planning. And it extends beyond the expert–client relationship and the making of recommendations, to encompass regulations, plans, and reports that, in their very existence, broadcast the moral basis for a city's development. To address this wider sense of prescribing, I consider three broad themes in this chapter. The first theme is the nagging problem of how to derive recommendations from technical analyses. Facts do not speak for themselves, but out of knowledge must come prescription. The second theme concerns what theorists have termed the ethics of planning and, specifically, the issue of professional behavior. In doing so, and similar to other planning theorists, I extend ethics into the realm of moral responsibilities as they relate to how planners engage broad social values, particularly justice. The third theme involves politics – specifically, the political ideologies that relate planning to the state, the economy, and civil society – and to power – and thereby serve as guidance for proposing what should be done.

4.1 From knowledge to prescription

No matter how robust the information, how sophisticated the analysis, or how incontrovertible the findings, the knowledge that emerges from planners' inquiries is still only a rudimentary guide to what might and should be done. Having finished the technical part of planning, what remains is the advice. But what to say? A planner could address the lack of affordable housing by having the government make more land available for residential construction; limit rents; subsidize home builders; provide financial support to lower-income households; finance, build, and manage social housing; expand and improve mass transit to allow people to live in less expensive communities and easily commute to their jobs; or all or combinations of the above. Many different responses are possible, any one of which would address the problem. But as the philosopher David Hume pointed out centuries ago, no clear path connects what "is" to what "ought" to be. The facts tell planners what conditions exist and what trends are underway. They do not tell them what to do to meliorate undesirable conditions or take advantage of opportunities. To develop their advice, planners have to bring values to bear or, to be more precise, they have to acknowledge the values hidden within the advice itself as well as the values they have ignored or suppressed (Campbell 2012; Watson 2006, 38). Whose values matter and how are they best realized?

In the formative years of city planning, a solution seemed to be at hand, one that joined democracy to the administration of things. During the period of urban reform in the late 19th and early 20th centuries, those proposing to establish planning within local governments believed that the role of planners was to provide technical advice to elected officials about how to manage the city. The objective was to run government on a scientific and even business-like basis thereby displacing the influence of "special" interests. Planning's advocates were not so naïve as to believe that interests, values, and political ideologies could be banished. Rather, technical understandings would temper them. Elected officials simply needed to be convinced to draw on the advice of experts. Reformers further hoped that these officials would use their understanding of what citizens valued to decide what issues needed to be addressed. Once a problem was defined and values set, a solution was a mere technical matter. Developed in this way, planning advice would be democratic by definition. In effect, a distinction was struck between factual knowledge and democratically informed, political knowledge, with planners the means-technicians to those who were democratically elected to express the "ends," or values, of the public. The is/ought problem would be resolved by a division of labor. As one planning scholar (Hoover 1961, 293) noted back in 1961, "the aims and directions of moral choice are 'policy' matters, not to be entrusted to experts." This resolution, though, cast planners as solely technocratic – itself a fiction – and was impractical in practice. It assumed that planners' observations and recommendations were value-free. From a theoretical perspective at least, the advice-giving problem remained.[1]

Charles Lindblom (1959) proposed a different solution in his discussion of incrementalism. He implied that planners struggled with what to recommend because they falsely believed that a best solution existed to be discovered: anything short of that was a failure. Lindblom encouraged planners to recognize the political dangers of proposing anything in excess of what was already being done. Advice that strayed beyond the boundaries of existing political compromises was bad advice. What planners needed to do was focus on initiatives already underway and on initiatives similar to them. By indicating what the public values, what is currently being done defines the limits of political feasibility. In effect, make incremental proposals for they are more likely to be adopted by elected officials. Or, said differently, avoid innovations for they are politically problematic. From Lindblom's perspective of ensuring that planners' recommendations are adopted, this makes sense. What it also does, as many of his critics pointed out, is yoke planners to the status quo; it seems inherently conservative. In his defense, Lindblom responded that no limit was placed on the pace of incremental change. To the extent that incrementalism blocks consideration of values not already adopted, it is only a partial solution to the is/ought conundrum.

A more promising response has involved the notion of the public interest. From the beginning of institutionalized planning, practitioners have believed that a public interest existed that overrode special interests. If the public interest could be discovered, then planners would know what advice to give. It would be the touchstone for their recommendations. Once facts were determined, knowledge of the public interest would enable planners to sift out inappropriate responses. If the public preferred subsidies to households rather than subsidies to developers to make housing affordable, then the advice to give to elected officials was clear. As importantly, having access to the public interest and thus speaking for the public would legitimize planning as a governmental activity (Moroni 2004). And, unlike Lindblom's call to act incrementally and unlike those who assign facts to planners and values to elected officials, it would buffer planners from political interference. "Serving the public" seemed an impenetrable defense.

Beginning approximately in the 1960s, however, the notion that a public interest could guide planners came under strong criticism (Klosterman 1980). No single, homogeneous public existed, critics argued. Interests were plural, not singular. Moreover, any claim to a public interest marginalized democratic governance: the existence of a public interest, uncovered by experts, whether planners or pollsters, seemed to make unnecessary a democracy in which people talked to each other. In addition, and most bothersome, those who championed the public interest were accused of lacking any systematic and defensible procedures for identifying it. The common approach has been to treat the public interest as an aggregation of individual interests, that is, to approach it from a utilitarian perspective. Within planning, this has usually meant involving residents in the planning process. Allowing people to speak, hearing of their concerns and preferences, gives planners a better sense of what to advise. But, as discussed previously, resident participation is an imperfect mechanism for engaging the public. Even a public brought together around a simple community concern is seldom in agreement and planners are left with only a murky understanding of what that public wants. Planners have also conducted surveys, utilized web-based tools, held "visioning" exercises, and, of course, relied on elected officials to identify the public interest, but have done so with no greater success.

While an aggregative sense of the public interest is common in planning, also important is planners' organic sense of the public interest. This is different. It is not a sum of individual interests (i.e., what people prefer) but what is deemed in the interest of the city and its residents as an organic entity. The question to ask when considering what to prescribe is "what would best enable the city to function efficiently and allow people to prosper?" For planners, the answer lies in their particular understanding of cities and regions; that is, it lies in their expertise and technical knowledge and not with the public. In effect, the organic public interest is centered on the ideal of a well-organized, well-functioning city. Consequently, the public interest is defined in terms of developmental consequences and is more substantive than procedural. In this organic state, it also privileges theories-in-planning over theories-of-planning.

As Susan Fainstein (2008, 70) has written: "The profession of urban planning was born of a vision of the good city." Planners have always had a sense of what a proper city should be, whether this was the utopias of the 19th century, the Garden City of the early 20th century, or the current fascination with sustainable, livable, and smart cities. These understandings have informed the plans they have written and the recommendations they have made. Where planning has maintained a link to architecture both academically and professionally, planners have had access to numerous versions of the ideal city. Often embedded in theories of urban form, such formulations can be used to bridge the gap between "is" and "ought." With the "good city" in mind, planners can sift through possible recommendations and select those most likely to lead to the intended result. An organic approach to the public interest thus enables planners to remain in control of their advice (resident participation and elected officials seemingly cast aside) and take responsibility for what they propose. One theorist (Tait 2016), rather than label this the public interest, has characterized it as planners' "transcendent interest."

Two groups of planning theorists are relevant here, one associated with theories of urban form and the other with political values, neither of whom are shy about prescribing the good city. The first are the New

Urbanists, primarily U.S. based but also found under the label of neo-traditionalists in the United Kingdom and other countries (Beauregard 2002). These theorists are essentially interested in urban forms that capture the physical sensibility of small towns and that encourage interaction among residents. For them, the point of planning and design is to contribute to a sense of community. Mainly focused on residential areas, they favor medium densities, less emphasis on accommodating the automobile, walkability, animated public spaces, and a textured architecture that evokes the past while connecting the private and semi-public realms.

The second group is made up of just-city theorists and their right-to-the-city associates. They too have a sense of what kinds of cities planners should prescribe. Concerned that procedural approaches evade planners' moral obligations and leave the just city undefined, they have been assertive in their substantive proposals. A good example comes from Susan Fainstein (2008). Her program for a just city includes public spaces that accommodate diverse groups, affordable housing, social mixing in neighborhoods, the public provision of social services including communal facilities, the encouragement of small businesses and cooperatives, "green" development and strong environmental regulations, mega-projects that respect the popular will and preserve the urban fabric, and a sensitivity to the quality of the city's architecture. In addition, she wants the details of these planning outcomes to be resolved through extensive citizen participation. Fainstein believes that a city with these qualities reflects the goals of a just planning: equality among residents, enhanced democracy, and tolerance for social differences. Approaching planning from this perspective, these theorists make their position explicit: the is/ought conundrum is resolved when planners recognize their political obligation to be progressive and plan for a just world. What is to be done is prescribed – and proscribed – by the values they embrace.

4.2   Ethics and morality

The task of prescribing, and specifically crafting advice out of knowledge, is not simply a matter of the directives of elected officials, recognition of the public interest, or the substantive and political interests of planners. It is also filtered through the ethical guidelines of right and wrong that are part of any profession and by the moral responsibilities that planners have as both planners and citizens. Recognizing this, and in reaction to the technocratic and apolitical stance of main-stream planners in the 1950s and early 1960s, a number of planning theorists began to question planners' ethical responsibilities. By the nature of their work, planners are compelled to make choices and take action, and their ethics, these theorists maintain, set boundaries on this behavior. Such choices involve more than technical calculations of effectiveness; they also entail distributional issues regarding who should benefit. Planners constantly address questions of "what should be done, for whom and by whom, and with what benefits or losses" (Watson 2003, 404). With the move away from a consensus-based planning to one more engaged with cultural differences and, for some theorists, deeply rooted conflicts, the ethical requirements on planners became amplified.

One of the paths of this inquiry led to professional ethics and matters of right and wrong. Planning is generally viewed as a profession, not an occupation, and as such has responsibilities that go beyond merely doing the job well. Like other professions such as medical doctors or lawyers, planners are presumed to be accountable to ethical guidelines that govern their professional behavior. Theorists thus set out to dis-cover the ethical issues faced by planners and how planners responded to them (Hendler 1991; Howe 1979). Various surveys identified three issues that preoccupied planners: transparency as regards planning data, truthfulness as regards relations with the community and elected officials, and the need to balance the demands made on them by elected officials (their putative clients) with those requiring them to attend to the public interest. These surveys also found that whereas planners were in agreement on certain core values (e.g., do not misinform, do not take bribes), there was less agreement on a variety of other issues (e.g., whether information could be leaked, whether issues could be dramatized to overcome public apathy, whether recommendations could be changed under political pressure). The Canadian planning scholar Sue Hendler (1996) concluded that these professional dilem-mas could best be understood by treating planning as enmeshed in competing responsibilities and multiple allegiances. Consequently, while ethical clarity might be achieved on some issues, it could not be achieved on all. Even if the profession publicized ethical guidelines, these principles still needed to be applied in specific situations and weighed against other and equally applicable principles. Would the public interest be served by sharing information with a community group outside normal channels or would it be harmed? Would doing so cause people to see planners as less than "objective"?

Casting ethical quandaries in this way and subsequently finding professional ethics to be a conceptual dead end, theorists began to explore other ways of thinking about ethics and morality. Hendler (1994) turned to feminist thought as a way of breaking out of the straitjacket of professional ethics and broadening her ethical gaze. Her goal was a planning ethics that would cover everything from the planner's moral responsibilities to everyday professional etiquette. At the core of this ethics would be a recognition of the relational nature of all human activity. For feminists, she noted, what matters is how we engage with others and the importance of doing so with respect and equanimity. To this, Hendler appended the emphasis on care in feminist thought. Doing so, she believed, would bolster a planning ethics resistant to oppression and distressed by the conditions in which disadvantaged people were forced to live – ethical positions well known within planning but not previously justified in this way. Her planning ethics was additionally to attend to the sexism expressed in how cities were organized, buildings designed, and homes arranged. Here is where planners could be particularly influential given their expertise. A feminist-inspired, ethical city, for example, would have ample day-care services and homes that did not isolate women in the kitchen. Hendler even extended her ethical reach to encompass the instrumental and utilitarian biases of planning techniques and the tendency of planners to favor rational, interest-based, and factual deliberations over emotional, anecdotal, and experiential speech. Here was an ethics less concerned with judging actions right or wrong, good or bad, and more with leading life in a particular, caring way.

Building in part on Hendler's writings, Heather Campbell developed an ethical theory around the notion of "situated ethical judgment" and the claim that ethical values are just the "starting point" for planning thought (Campbell 2002). Rather than pursue ethical principles that have universal applicability, Campbell instead focused on the ethical choices faced in specific situations and made with and for others. Planners, she maintained, always acted in settings where they were constantly valuing and re-evaluating actions and outcomes; they were not imposing universal values or pursuing utopian ideals. The planner's task was to negotiate among contending interests in a way that balanced freedom and individual rights with collective obligations. Concerned that this approach would be read as wholly procedural and agnostic as regards outcomes and therefore insufficient for acting ethically, Campbell introduced a substantive and moral dimension to her argument. Drawing on the premise that society expects its public institutions to be just and to treat everyone equally, she argued that justice has to be central to planners' ethical judgments (Campbell 2006). Planning judgments will be accepted to the extent that they are reasonable and just.[2]

Clearly, this is not a narrowly procedural argument. Campbell is explicit regarding the need for planning processes to be supplemented with a substantive commitment to social justice. Justice, though, has to be cast in collective rather than individualistic terms. The justice she wants planners to embrace recognizes the social nature of human existence, acknowledges differences, and extends beyond those with whom planners share a common identity. She taps the deep roots of planning to write that "reasoning and justice are inescapably linked" (Campbell 2006, 102). And although her focus on the thin value of justice seems incompatible with a dismissal of universal values as the key to planning ethics, she nevertheless recognizes that an ethical planning cannot ignore its substantive outcomes, even if justice is a weak guide. Her solution: justice has to be situated, that is, understood and applied in specific contexts.

The search for guiding principles has its roots in a well-known article by the former Columbia University planning professor, Peter Marcuse (1976). (His choice, then, was equity and democracy.) In that piece, Marcuse dismissed a planning ethics that focused solely on professional behavior. That approach, he argued, privileged allegiance to the client, guild loyalty, statutory responsibilities, and the advancement of knowledge. For Marcuse, this was system-maintaining and much too narrow an ethical agenda. What mattered instead were planners' social and moral responsibilities beyond workplace relations. Writing during the years when the United States was experiencing significant popular unrest around civil rights, women's liberation, environmental degradation, and opposition to the U.S. involvement in Vietnam, Marcuse encouraged planners to take a stance on these issues and do so both in and outside their professional lives. Admittedly, planners as governmental employees are constrained in how they can protest the war or nuclear disarmament, but they do have ways of resisting housing discrimination, fighting poverty, and championing environmental protection.

As, if not more, serious for Marcuse was the obligation planners had as citizens to speak out and act on issues that existed beyond their professional realm. They did not leave morality behind when they joined the profession. Ethics did not stop at the technical limits of practice; it extended to a questioning of "the functions the profession serves, the tasks it is assigned" (Marcuse 1976, 272). In effect, it extended beyond functional rationality. A truly engaged and ethical planner, Marcuse asserted, would recognize the conservative bias of professional planning and the harm that it can do. What needed to be acknowledged was how economic and political power mediated professional activities and threatened equity and democracy. The ethical planner was to be system-challenging rather than system-maintaining.

Marcuse's argument reflected the then-emergence of advocacy planning as well as the notion that not only was planning political in its formulations and consequences, but that planners were political beings obliged to recognize and apply the values they embraced. Political values should guide a planner's ethical judgments. The assumption of Marcuse and the advocacy planners was that regardless of whether planners were politically progressive, centrist, or reformist, they would willingly endorse democracy, equality, and justice as ethical principles. That planners might be conservative or interpret these principles in a less-than-progressive fashion was unthinkable. To this extent, progressive theorists turned back to universal values, but did so in a way that treated them as emerging from what can be termed a Left ideological position. Only these values, applied in the ways they imagined them to be, constituted ethical planning. All else, for example planning that attempted to maximize choices in the market (favoring individual freedom over collective advancement), was, by implication, unethical. This position reflects the reformist leanings of planning theorists and a blindness to a conservative planning.

One moral principle – justice – currently looms large in the theory literature. The key text here is Susan Fainstein's *The Just City* (2010), in which justice is defined in terms of democracy, equity, and diversity. Guiding planning ethics should be the goals of making collective decision-making public and inclusive, distributing the benefit of public policies in ways that favor those who are least advantaged (following the philosopher John Rawls's justice-as-fairness approach), and ensuring that the differences between groups of people are respected and not used to treat them inequitably. Planners should strive for a city devoid of injustice, that is, devoid of "actions that disadvantage those who already have less or who are excluded from entitlements enjoyed by others who are no more deserving" (2010, 30). By implication, a just planning is an ethical planning. Moreover, Fainstein claims that justice can be conceived in such a way as to fall within the city government's mandate, a critical assumption for any theorist who wishes to influence planning practice.

This just-city argument has been criticized by the American scholar Robert Lake (2016). Rejecting subject–object dualisms, he accuses the "just-city" theorists of erroneously presenting justice as "the object of planning, the normative end that planning practice should be designed, organized, and implemented to achieve" (p. 1205). This, he claims, situates justice within the confines of a solely substantive approach to planning and falls victim to a false distinction between process and outcome. In its place, he proposes what he terms planning *with* justice, not planning *for* justice. Planning with justice better comports with a pragmatism that rejects foundationalism, is anticipatory and generative, embraces contingency, and is democratically inclusive. Justice is not introduced into the world of planners "after the fact," as one might add a consideration of gender to a theory of residential choice, but is integral to planning from the beginning. Justice should pervade everything one does as a planner and must be seen as both a means and an end. Planning is one way to practice justice and bring it into existence.

Agreeing with Lake that too much emphasis is given either to procedures or to outcomes, the Dutch planning theorist Claudia Basta (2016) urges planning theorists to break from approaches to ethics that are attached to how plans are made or what plans do to people. She is particularly uncomfortable with formulations that extrapolate from Rawls's justice-as-fairness argument with its emphasis on equal rights, the distribution of social and economic inequalities to benefit those who are least advantaged, and the opening of offices and positions to all people. She maintains that Rawls fails to consider people's ability to take advantage of these opportunities. Basta thus turns to the capabilities approach associated with the philosopher Martha Nussbaum and the economist Amartya Sen (Fainstein 2010, 54–56). Nussbaum and Sen propose that justice is achieved only to the extent that people can realize the life they value. This involves being and having: being in good health, being able to earn an income, having shelter, having loving relationships. The goal of planning should be to enhance the ability of people to do these things, that is, to make them capable of living well. And although Basta acknowledges that much of this would fall outside the formal responsibilities of public planning, she sees no barriers to planners collaborating with others to achieve this goal.

Given their arguments, Basta and Lake would likely reject the claim that the ethical destination of planning should be a "right-to-the-city" (Marcuse 2009). The right-to-the-city argument is somewhat distinct from the just-city position. Rather than justice, which seems to be wholly focused on substantive outcomes, the right-to-the-city idea entails "an exigent demand by those deprived of basic material and existing legal rights, and an aspiration for the future by those discontented with life as they see it around them, perceived as limiting their own potentials for growth and creativity" (Marcuse 2009, 190). Peter Marcuse, one of its major proponents, means it as a moral claim not a legal claim. It entails a bundle of rights: to public space, information, transparency in government, adequate housing. The focus is hence shifted from the substantive and reformist outcomes of a just-city approach to Constitutional possibilities and social capabilities. Opportunities have to be made widely available and people have to be able to take advantage of them when they arise. In these right-to-the-city arguments, however, what planners might do is unclear. If providing more choices to those lacking moral and political standing is the response to this criticism, it is far from sufficient to guide planners in their ethical judgments.

Unacknowledged in this discussion – Marcuse being the exception – is the ethical responsibility planners have for the harm and disruption caused by planning. Lisa Schweitzer (2016), a U.S. planning theorist, is even more emphatic than Marcuse. She states what almost all formulations of planning ethics have suppressed: planning institutions impose unwanted change on people. They allow and even encourage commercial districts to invade adjacent residential areas, remove on-street parking spaces to plant trees and set down street furniture, and reroute bus lines to make the transit system more efficient. In these and other instances, some people benefit and others are harmed, and this harm is part of planners' ethical responsibilities. Moreover, Schweitzer claims, harm is something that can be addressed within the world of professional planning (see also Marris 1975).

In developing her position, Schweitzer begins with the idea of therapeutic imagination proposed by Leonie Sandercock to address the healing necessitated by disruptions to a community. Her concern is not with therapy and psychological matters, though, but rather with people's attachment to the political community and how that attachment can be, might need to be, restored. Planned disruptions have the potential to weaken and even sever political ties. And while a disruption might cause harm, it might not always be a wrong, that is, ethically problematic and damaging of political relationships. When it does cause wrongful harm, atoning actions that re-establish and strengthen the political community have to be undertaken. Compensation and restitution, however, are insufficient. If households have been forcefully displaced by a highway project, it is not enough to pay their moving expenses. In these circumstances, people feel marginalized: they feel they have been deemed insignificant. What is needed is "credible commitments to reform that prevent future harms and wrongs" (Schweitzer 2016, 141; see also Moroni 2010a). Schweitzer thus goes beyond Sandercock's call for healing. She extends planners' responsibilities to the reform of institutional politics. For her, atoning is simply a way "to disperse with, move on from, or preempt the tarnishing of institutions" (p. 141) and for that reason should be avoided. Atoning is a system-maintaining response.

As regards ethics and morality, planning theorists can be divided into those who believe that ethical judgments should proceed from situated engagements and deliberations and those who view planning as decidedly progressive and thus feel compelled to deploy a left-leaning political agenda.[3] For the latter, the turn to pragmatic inquiry is nothing but an avoidance of what should be done. More blurred than precise, this distinction nonetheless points to the importance of politics and ideology to the prescribing in which planners engage. In fact, all these theorists agree that planning is political, that planners themselves have politics, and that no choice is devoid of values. The question is to what degree their politics do and should guide their prescriptions.

4.3   From politics to prescription

Beginning with its adoption by the local governments of liberal democracies, planning has been reformist in intent. Consequently, it occupies a centrist position on the spectrum of political ideologies. Most planners neither want to preserve society as it is nor radically transform it. Their goal is improvement. And, because these planners generally reject political ideologies (partly a consequence of their technocratic leanings) and retain an attachment to the public interest, they view planning as falling outside the realm of partisan politics, despite being political.[4] To improve society, to make cities and regions function better according to their organic tendencies, is to make everyone's life better.

Of course, this is a delusion. Because planning is done through the state, because societies are composed of people with different needs and interests, and because the choices available to elected officials and the city's residents are never ideal, planning is uneven in its consequences; it serves some groups and not others, even as the distribution of benefits shifts over time. Much of the politics of planning, in fact, revolves around its positioning within the state. This relationship has a great deal to do with the issues planners address and the advice they give, as numerous critics from the political left and the political right have pointed out. At the extremes of political criticism, governmental planning is rejected. The far Left argues for replacing governmental planning with insurgent planning; the extreme Right embraces a market wholly unfettered – free – of planning regulations. Of course, authoritarian governments do adopt planning, though mainly because it coordinates development with the dictates of the regime, not because it can institute reform. (Reform can be dangerous.) Permeating all these issues is power, a resource that planners would like to possess in order to do good and yet, at the same time, blame for their inability to make the improvements they deem necessary. Undeniable is that political ideology, whether imposed by the state or adopted by planners, is a major influence on the prescriptions of government.

The canonical story of planning's contemporary origins tells of planners' emergence in response to the dire physical conditions and human misery of the industrial city (Hall 2002, 13–47). An emerging middle class spawned a group consisting of a variety of erstwhile reformers concerned with public health, housing, child labor, and congestion (Spain 2001, 30–60) along with a parallel group of reformers concerned that the chaos of the industrial city was stifling commerce (Boyer 1983). The first concerned themselves with the plight of the poor and – in the United States – with immigrants, the second with business and the chaos of the industrial city's built environment. One group was driven by Christian charity and the other group by a belief in progress and economic growth. Lurking on the margins were activists who targeted the abysmal conditions under which people labored, a concern too of economic elites who feared labor unrest. For the most part, the history of planning's origins focuses on its reformist inclinations. In addition, planners were intent on bringing about what was then labeled "good government" and this also reinforced the sense that planning was apolitical and non-partisan.

The commitment to apolitical improvement continues to the present. Most planners view their task as making the city a better place for all people, whether it is protecting the city against sea-level rise, improving the flow of freight traffic, building affordable housing, or expanding access to open space. Even a Left planning theorist such as Susan Fainstein embraces this reformist position, though with a caveat. In an article written with Norman Fainstein on a Marxist perspective on planning, they admonished radical planners for ignoring the fact that "the better the better" (Fainstein and Fainstein 1979). They wrote: "To the extent that planning furthers the material situation of the lower classes it is progressive, even if it legitimizes the system in the short run" (p. 399). Fainstein's recent book, *The Just City* (2010), echoes this when she calls for more justice regardless of the institutional forms necessary to achieve it, that is, regardless of whether the capitalist system is left intact. This is hardly a rejection of reform. The caveat is that her preference is for non-reformist reforms that contribute to long-run structural change rather than reinforcing existing injustices (Fainstein 2010, 17–20). As another illustration of the grip of reformism on planning, Bish Sanyal (2002), professor of planning at MIT and as progressive in his outlook as Fainstein, takes the position that, in democratic societies, planners will be effective to the extent that they engage in compromise. Planners should be reasonable; they should be politically practical. Like good centrists, they should avoid moral absolutes and listen to what people think. Neither Fainstein nor Sanyal, then, rejects reform. Although both might bristle at being labeled centrists, their arguments support reform as an appropriate political stance for planners.[5]

Not everyone views planning as centrist and thus reformist. A few planning scholars have pro-market tendencies and believe planning to be insufficiently attentive to what they see as its primary role of enabling the functioning of the free market (Allmendinger 2009, 105–127; Taylor 1998, 130–154). For even more conservative thinkers, planning is a threat to individual freedom and specifically property rights (Frick 2013). Within the planning theory literature, the figure of ill repute here is Friedrich Hayek (1944), who attacked planning in the late 1940s for being a step on the path to authoritarian socialism. Hayek asserted that planning can only be successful, though detrimental to society, on its own terms. This means centralizing power in the hands of a powerful bureaucracy and a few people. Planning takes freedoms away from individual investors, businesses, and households and fuels the expansion of an oppressive state. And while the taint of socialism is every so often used to denigrate planning, this is an issue that was "of its time" and attracts little attention from planning theorists today.

Of greater concern for contemporary planning theorists is neoliberalism, a political ideology that ostensibly threatens planning's progressive possibilities (Campbell, Tait, and Watkins 2014). Neoliberal thought asserts the dominance of neoclassical economic thinking while extending market principles to all aspects of collective life. Regulations are to be limited to those whose economic benefits exceed their economic costs, citizens are to be treated as apolitical consumers of public services, and governments are to be reimagined as public entrepreneurs rather than caretakers of the public realm. At best, such a perspective marginalizes planners and, at worst, turns them into just another market actor. The liberal project of planning with its concern for reform and the common good is consequently stifled. What is needed, the U.S. planning theorist Ananya Roy (2008, 100) asserts, is a post-liberal planning that engages in a moral struggle with the world of politics thereby resisting neoliberalism and advancing a "moral, restrained, and empathetic [liberal self], searching for norms of public conduct and transaction."

Further to the Left on planning's political spectrum are the critics of planning's reformist bent. They accuse planners of being merely a tool of capitalism, not the harbinger of socialism as did Hayek. Their complaints focus on planners' institutional position within the state. For the most part, these dissenting views come from the Marxist political left. David Harvey (1978), the well-known Marxist geographer, spoke to this line of attack in a 1978 article that began with the premise that the state is essentially another mechanism by which the capitalist class rules. Consequently, the overall function of the state is to enhance and protect the capitalist project. One of the ways it does this is through its planning apparatus, whose main task is to organize the built environment to support investment and commerce. This means providing such collective infrastructure as roads, bridges, and water supply systems that no individual capitalist will build, arranging roads and rail lines so that goods can flow easily and cheaply, supporting the social needs of labor (e.g., low-cost housing) to head off unrest and allow wages to be kept low, and generally intervene when capitalism erupts into one of its frequent crises (e.g., a collapse of central city land values caused by capital flight). From a Marxist perspective, what planners prescribe always emanates from their subordination to the capitalist state. Harvey does recognize the persistence of planners' progressive (and thus reformist) roots that commit it to the "ideology of social harmony" and "defender of the public interest" (p. 224). Still, limits exist and those limits rise when planners threaten the reproduction of the capitalist order.[6]

M. Christine Boyer (1983), an architectural and planning historian working in the United States, also embedded planning within the state's relationship to capitalism, but from a perspective inspired by the French theorist Michel Foucault rather than Karl Marx. She too argued that planning and the state are concerned with the spatial order of the city. Her theoretical contribution was in casting this in disciplinary terms. The purpose of planning is to discipline the city's built environment. This means ordering it such a way that it supports both the reproduction of capital and the reproduction of labor. The city, she wrote, is "an instrument of capitalist development" (p. 66) and planners are the supervisors of that instrument. The implication, as with Harvey, is that the politics of planners are the politics of the capitalist class. Planners' prescriptions embody and cannot escape the interests of the state.

A line of critique related to this "state capture" approach and reminiscent of Hayek's accusation that planning is a mechanism for total control involves the way in which planning loses all its reformist and progressive tendencies when embedded within authoritarian states. Two nations to note here are South Africa and Israel, states in which planning has been used in support of state oppression. In South Africa, under the apartheid regime that existed from 1948 to 1994, planners were complicit in keeping the black population impoverished and separate from the white population and its privileges (Beauregard 1998; Mabin and Smit 1997). They designed townships that were exclusively for blacks, used highways and industrial areas to isolate these places, and passed regulations to prohibit blacks from occupying white neighborhoods. The goal was to keep the cities "white by night." Blacks could be employed in the cities during the day as servants and factory workers, but had to leave when their workday was done. When they traveled to their townships for the night, they did so on the roads and rail lines that had been planned especially for this. In Israel, the group is different but the role of the planners similar (Yiftachel 1996). There, the planners have used roadways and physical barriers to isolate Arabs from the Jewish population. They have also contributed to the extension of the Jewish presence into Arab areas through the planning and design of Jewish settlements. Here is what some scholars (Yiftachel

1998) label the "noir" side of planning, a label that points to the malleability of planning in relationship to state politics and ideology. And, while governmental planners in both countries have exhibited concern for the groups being segregated, the overall thrust of their work, their critics maintain, has been to inscribe apartheid on the land.

Much less extreme in their evaluation of the politics of state planning are the progressives within planning theory, a category so flexible as to include both centrists and reformed Marxists. From a radical perspective, progressives are the reformists, but reform is just the beginning for progressives. The objective is to push past what has already been accomplished and to do more: to provide more justice, to establish a right-to-the-city. The American planning theorist Pierre Clavel (1986) argued that to be truly progressive required a progressive local government. He documented a number of instances of what he termed progressive planning, and in all of them a political coalition and/or mayor had been elected that was committed to shifting the focus of planning from business and the downtowns to the neighborhoods, from growth to distribution and environmental sustainability, and from those who were doing well to those who had fewer opportunities. These local governments also increased the involvement of residents in policymaking. The theoretical point here is that when planners are embedded in the state, the political inclinations of the state set the boundaries on what they can prescribe.

For this reason, a number of theorists have called for an insurgent planning that empowers marginalized and oppressed groups and is situated outside of and most often in opposition to the state, similar to an earlier advocacy planning (Friedmann 1992; Miraftab 2009). Their world is that of civil society, not the state. Concerned that injustice, inequality, cultural imperialism, and violence can rarely be overcome through state policies, they call instead for planners to engage with popular movements whose aim is to transform and even replace the state. Insurgent planners join rent strikes, engage in labor organizing, support women's activism and environmental movements, participate in anti-globalization demonstrations, favor immigrant support and anti-violence campaigns, and become part of highly politicized activities that empower local groups and communities. Drawing on planning's tradition of social mobilization described by John Friedmann (1987, 225–308), insurgent planning is committed to "structural changes in the very society that the social reform tradition, with its paternalistic ethos, is trying to build up" (p. 297).

But what actually does the radical planner offer such movements? If the empowerment of marginalized peoples is one of the goals of all radical action, what do planners contribute? In situations of state reform, the planning role is relatively clear – technical advice is needed to manage and reform the city. Insurgent planning requires a different style of prescribing, or the abandonment of the prescriptive task altogether. Insurgencies are not always non-violent, they are not always willing to compromise, and they are not wholly concerned with state policies particularly when a need exists to make major changes in social and cultural relations. But planners are not trained to provide advice in highly politicized settings in which activism and political strategy have to take precedence over rational calculation. In these circumstances, the prescriptions that planners might offer seem superfluous.

The emphasis on empowerment turns our attention to the issue of power, specifically planners' capacity to mobilize people and resources to act in certain ways and not others, and their opponents' capacity to block these efforts.[7] Power has haunted planners from its institutionalized beginnings. The early Progressive Era reformers in the United States looked to the state for funds, legal support, and administrative legitimacy. Planning would be supported by state power. Believing that they could institute good government, they would also be able to resist the power of special interests. Later, planners came to realize that state support was not automatic and that they needed to influence political leaders: good advice alone was insufficient for obtaining political support. Knowledge was not necessarily power. Rather than develop their persuasive talents, advocacy and insurgent planners turned to alterative centers of power outside the state. Popular mobilizations, they decided, could provide the necessary capacity for bringing about the change that these radical planners deemed necessary and appropriate. To the extent that action is the point of planning and, consequently, has to be addressed by theorists, the meaning and presence (or absence) of power is unavoidable (Hoch 1984b). Take into consideration two examples, one from the Danish planning theorist Bent Flyvbjerg and the other from the debate around communicative practice.

Flyvbjerg's *Rationality and Power* (1998), discussed previously, explores the conditions under which planners can be successful in their prescriptions. For him, the issue is the extent to which knowledge (meaning good technical advice cast in terms of the public interest) is sufficient for obtaining the consent of elected officials and the necessary legal and financial resources for effectuating that advice. What he found in his observation of the planners in Aalborg, Denmark, was that when plans and recommendations were unacceptable to the local business community, they were easily thwarted. The reasonable and technically informed justifications planners put forth wilted under the political pressure of local business elites who had access to and influence over local officials that planners lacked. They could mount criticisms and offer perspectives that no amount of technical scrutiny could overcome. In short, power dispenses with knowledge, turning rationality into rationalization. Such a conclusion, of course, goes against the grain of much planning thought. To be fair, Flyvbjerg was simply repeating what many planning theorists, and particularly radical planners, believe. Planning is successful – its prescriptions adopted – to the extent that it has access to either popular or institutional power. When it lacks such access, it fails.[8]

As a second example of this theoretical concern with power, consider the disagreement between theorists (the seeming majority) who support procedural approaches to planning theory and those who argue for more substantive approaches (Fainstein 2000, 453–461; Hoch 1984a; Huxley and Yiftachel 2000). While the latter criticize the former for leaving unspoken what the material consequences of planning might be, an equally frequently made criticism is that communicative practice and other process-oriented theorists (including the pragmatists) forget that power is unequally distributed across people and organizations (Abram 2000). The capacity to influence deliberations and to implement, even to the point of blocking widespread agreement, varies in ways that are unavoidable and significant in their consequences. Collaboration and deliberation can easily be transformed into fruitless exercises by powerful individuals and groups who have interests different from what has been consensually decided and who have privileged access, as in Flyvbjerg's study, to decision-makers. Procedural theorists assume that people can be reasonable and are either equally powerful or willing to suppress the power they have in service of a democratic process. This strikes these critics as naïve. Their response is to focus on what, substantively, should be done and then to consider how it can be made to happen. If this entails going outside the state to join with popular oppositions, then so be it. For them, prescription comes first; strategizing about power follows.

4.4 Conclusion

In order to prescribe, in order to craft and convey the advice that is expected of them and to decide for themselves what is the moral thing to do, planners have to recognize the inherent normativity of their endeavor. Technical understandings are only the starting point for being able to say what should be done. Value perspectives are also required and this means going well beyond professional ethics. It requires a sense of what matters to whom and how others can be convinced to take this into account. Planning theorists, though, split among those who counsel democratic procedures, whether it be a search for the public interest or a pragmatic and collaborative consensus; those who point to the core values of justice, democracy, and equity as guides to advice-giving; and those who call for planners to embrace the precepts of a progressive, and even radical, political ideology. In all these instances, and for the great majority of planners who work in government, the state looms over what they prescribe. To an uncomfortable degree, the values espoused by the state are the values that govern planners. Politics rules. Even an insurgent planning, ostensibly freed from state controls, does not escape the activist politics with which it is associated. Planners are never free of the many ways in which power and knowledge are intertwined.

Given these circumstances, what should planners do? How should they act? Is it enough to know, engage, and prescribe? If planning is meant to change the world, and change it for the better, should planners be doing more than telling others what to do? These questions point to the final of our four tasks – executing.

NOTES

1   This particular separation of facts and values has a parallel in what Corburn (2005) calls a compensatory approach to local knowledge, in which residents are brought into the planning process to comment on values and fairness and resolution of the issue is left to the planners.

2   Sanyal (2002) offers a friendly amendment: planners have to wade into ethical debates but also be willing to strike compromises as long as these compromises are transparent and substantively good.

3   Harper and Stein (1992) suggest even more complexity. They point to different approaches – utilitarianism, communitarianism, Rawlsian arguments – to ethics and the way in which advocating for a planning theory entails an underlying normative ethical theory.

4   Gunder (2010a) offers an insightful response to this position, as does Rabinovitz (1969) from a different theoretical perspective.

5   Worth mentioning is that one group's reform is another group's intrusion. Reform itself is a political ideology. Also worth noting is that, in practice, centrism has a bias for a procedural rather than consequentialist approaches to planning.

6 Fogelsong (1986) and Roweis (1981) developed similar arguments.
7 Metzger, Soneryd, and Hallström (2017) offer an insightful alternative to this hydraulic conception of power.
8 For Flyvbjerg, this is a depressing conclusion given his belief that modern democracy relies on rationality, not power, to work.

5 Executing

The planning literature is replete with categories. Academic planners write about *stages* of the planning process, *degrees* of citizen participation, *ways* of advice-giving, and *types* of plans. Planning has always been associated with a need to bring order to the world and one of the ways that it does so is by being analytical: distinguishing one thing from another and drawing boundaries between them. To plan in this fashion is to discipline a messy reality by putting things in their place. Of course, planning itself is bounded: it is itself a category. Planning began historically when superstition and faith were displaced by reason. It ends practically when advice is given and other people take the responsibility of doing what they have agreed should be done. Semantically speaking, planning precedes action, a formulation expressed in numerous distinctions between advisors and clients, staff and operating agencies, experts and decision-makers. But while the purported beginning is relatively uncontested, the ostensible conclusion is not.

To think of planning as ending after advice has been given or a plan proposed is to imagine a limit to planners' social responsibility and to establish the point at which planners can claim that they should no longer be held accountable.[1] This seems not just arbitrary but morally suspect. Most planners are governmental employees who perform a public service. To terminate their responsibility at advice-giving or plan-making seems to absolve them of the consequences of their actions. It strips them of moral agency. Contrarily, and to paraphrase the political philosopher Iris Marion Young (2011), when the actions of planners contribute to conditions and processes with which they and others live, they share responsibility for them. Those responsible are further obliged "to join with others who share that responsibility" (p. 96) such that any injustice or harm that has been done is rectified. This is what moral agents, acting politically, do.

This semantic boundary of planning perplexes many theorists. Widely recognized is that a particular category of action exists that is different from knowing, engaging, and prescribing. This "other" action pushes at planning's semantic limits and, if engaged, extends planners' responsibility to ensuring that the consequences they intend are realized. This I call "executing," that is, bringing into effect the consequences that flow from advice-giving and plan-making. Also termed implementation, executing is generally viewed, the Israeli planning theorist Rachel Alterman (1982, 228) notes, as a distinct step occurring after policy has been made or a plan adopted. In fact, in the rational-comprehensive model, planning ended with the adoption of the plan, its implementation being taken for granted (Alexander 1998).

Within the literature, many theorists argue for pushing beyond this ostensible boundary. One group is concerned with implementation, the other – the more politically radical – with social activism. Both question whether planners should confine themselves simply to ensuring that plans and advice are adopted. For them, implementation should not be an action independent of and subsequent to planning (Faludi 1973, 279). Rather, it should be incorporated as an extension of the planning process and thus part of planners' responsibility. Doing so, however, means engaging politically, an activity that planners have historically resisted and embraced only reluctantly. From their initial incorporation into government, planners have opted out of overt political engagement that might stray from acting rationally and reasonably, believing that their advice is defensible solely in terms of technical arguments. Despite that, many planners (theorists and practitioners alike) would agree that being apolitical has stymied their effectiveness and falsely represented their responsibilities. Nevertheless, to use coercion, intimidation, influence-peddling, and the trading of favors to achieve their ends – to be seriously and strategically political – strikes at the core of planning as scientific, reasonable, and reformist (Flyvbjerg 1998).

5.1   Implementation

It would not be too bold to assert that since planning's adoption by local governments, planners have been preoccupied with whether or not their advice is taken and their plans implemented. They want what they propose to come to fruition. But it is one thing to fret over this and another thing to do something about it. Two hurdles have to be navigated once planning, in its narrow sense, has been completed: decision-makers have to be convinced to accept and adopt what planners have proposed and, then, they have to allocate people and resources to implement it. Both have to occur for the consequences of planning to be realized.

The communicative turn in planning theory brought a theoretical sensibility to these two tasks. In recognition of the extent to which planning seems ineffective and its proposals unheeded, these theorists put forth the argument that good technical analysis by itself was insufficient (Forester 1989; Throgmorton 2000). Planners needed to be not just right but persuasive as well, with that persuasion relying mainly on the evidence at hand, that is, rhetorical without being deceptive. After they have determined what advice to give, written a report, or crafted a plan, they then have to develop arguments that convince clients and other decision-makers to adopt their proposals. To do otherwise is to conceive of planning in too constricted a sense. To assume that all people are swayed by a combination of evidence, technical logic, and scientific reasoning is a weak basis on which to build effectiveness. Rather, planners have to extend themselves into the social and political realm where decisions are made about which advice to take and whether or not plans should be adopted. They can do this by connecting reasonable arguments to the interests of those who have the power to command resources and act. In effect, they have to act politically. The objective is to couch high-quality advice in terms that appeal to clients without violating either the integrity of the analysis or the strictures of honest and transparent communication. Planners are not to deceive or threaten, but rather to mix evidence-based arguments with common sense and political realities. Although persuasion was intended to extend planning beyond its semantic limits, it was concerned more with adoption than implementation. A similar reluctance appears in the planning literature on implementation.

One group of theorists addresses implementation obliquely by asking what conditions must exist for plans to be considered effective. Their interest is more with being consequential than with generating specific consequences. Theirs is not a reflection on outcomes. The argument starts with two observations. The first is that planning has often been blamed (seemingly unfairly) for a variety of ills associated with urban development: sterile environments, traffic congestion, the paucity of affordable housing, sprawl. The second is that for planning to remain legitimate as a governmental activity, it has to demonstrate that it can be effective at producing the consequences that it claims are necessary and desirable. To defend itself and to maintain political support, the

U.S. theorist Emily Talen (1996) has written, more attention has to be given to developing a body of theory about why and how planning succeeds, even while recognizing that success is not an all-or-nothing proposition but an outcome adaptive to changing relationships, conditions, and understandings. In response to this challenge, these theorists have turned to the issue of plan evaluation and searched for answers to a single question: under what conditions are plans successful? The premise is that if planners know the factors that influence the success or failure of plans, they can act to ensure that those factors, when beneficial, are in place.

The approach taken is to divide the relevant factors into two categories: contextual factors and factors internal to planning (Laurien et al. 2004; Talen 1997). (The implication is that the latter are more susceptible to manipulation than the former.) Contextual factors include the degree of political support from elected officials, the extent of a city's pro-growth ideology (a pro-growth coalition is considered to be inclined to sacrifice planning concerns for the maximization of new investment), the level of community activism, and the availability of legal and regulatory support for planning. Internal factors include the resources available to the planning agency, the agency's organizational capacity, the quality of the plan (i.e., whether it meets technical and professional criteria), the size and complexity of the project, the inclination and ability of the planners to engage with developers and elected officials, and the quality of public review and participation. One empirical study (Laurien et al. 2004) of local plans in New Zealand identified five factors that were highly correlated with successful plan implementation: the quality of the plan, the capacity of the planning agency, the project scale, the actions of developers and consultants, and the quality of the interactions between planners and developers. In effect, it revealed a mix of contextual and internal factors. The authors ended the study by calling for improving the quality of plans and enhancing the implementation capacity of planning agencies. The former turns planners inward and back to their technical roots and is internal to planning; the latter is external in that it requires government funding for additional personnel and new computational capacity.

These theorists are fully aware that any approach to plan evaluation and any success depends on what kind of planning planners are doing (Baer 1987). For example, if a plan is meant to be a vision, then it will deal in broad generalizations and be difficult to evaluate. If it is considered a guide to the concerns that should be taken into account when making development and land-use decisions, it will pose a slightly more manageable evaluation problem. If planning is "a process for creating a frame of reference for operational decisions" (Alexander and Faludi 1989), with plans existing only to be helpful, then the evaluation should probably substitute a concern for process for a concern for outcomes. If the plan is conceived of and written as a blueprint, then its intended outcomes will be clear and an evaluation relatively easy. All of this becomes moot if plans are thought of as simply stories planners tell each other and non-planners rather than scientific statements about how the city should evolve. As stories, plans become just one of the many elements filtering through the ongoing discussions that are constantly occurring within any community (Throgmorton 2000). Of course, if this is the case, and planners want to influence how people understand the issues facing the city, they have to learn how to tell better stories.

Even if researchers identify the factors that determine a plan's success, the issue still remains as to how planners can ensure that those factors are in place. This need to influence the conditions in which planning is done and the capacity of planners to manage those conditions rests on the power and control that planners have. And if the capacity is determined to be insufficient, how it can be increased. The Dutch planning theorist Andreas Faludi (1973) recognized quite early in his career, and in the history of planning theory, that implementation was an essential, although frequently ignored, responsibility. What prevented planners from executing their plans was a lack of power that exacerbated their uncertainty about the future. For him, power would allow planners to control both contextuating factors and prescriptive factors, a distinction he borrowed from Amitai Etzioni, who contributed the idea of "mixed-scanning" to planning. Contextuating control entails being able to set a framework such that those meant to respond to the plan act in conformance with it. The goal is to limit responses to those that produce the intended consequences. Prescriptive control focuses on the particularities of what these actors do. Here, the planner shifts from setting the bounds on behavior to dictating specific behaviors. Faludi further noted that control could be coercive, utilitarian (e.g., providing material incentives), or persuasive and that the amount of control planners had depended on the resources at their disposal. He and the other theorists concerned with plan evaluation as a pathway to implementation success are silent, however, on how to obtain resources and translate them into control and influence over the factors associated with effectiveness.

Still deficient in this regard, but more helpful in revealing what has to be done so that plans are properly implemented, is the "classic" book – succinctly titled *Implementation* – on the topic by two U.S. policy scholars, Jeffrey Pressman and Aaron Wildavsky (1973). Pressman and Wildavsky present implementation as a form of joint action based on convincing participants to commit over an extended time to one or more of the many tasks and agreements involved in a project. For a project to be successful, people and organizations must be recruited and then kept in place, that is, their commitments maintained as the project unfolds. Although technical calculations and relationships are important (what was described above as the quality of the plan), even more consequential is ensuring that implementation is not delayed and that, if delayed, the various participants do not drift away to engage other obligations. The more a project experiences delay and the more the flow of decisions and tasks in the project is interrupted, the less likely the project will be realized. Delay is the enemy of successful implementation. Not only does delay breed delay, but small delays can accumulate and breed longer delays. As delays mount, the probability of the project being completed is diminished. Implicit in this argument is that statutory and contractual relations are insufficient for ensuring commitment to timely implementation. Other kinds of relationships have to be developed. In addition, decisions must be made and tasks performed so as not to threaten the fragility of the expectations held by the participants. Failure to do this will bring about the "slow dissolution of agreement" (p. 92). Planners must not only be flexible during implementation; they also need to set aside time and resources (i.e., create organizational slack) to adjust and adapt to changing circumstances. Pressman and Wildavsky suggest that, during the planning phase, planners should analyze the length and complexity of decision sequences embedded within the implementation process and use their findings to anticipate probable difficulties. In short, planners should attend to "the creation of organizational machinery for executing a program" (p. 144).

Pressman and Wildavsky's contribution was to cast implementation as an interlocking set of decision sequences carried out by multiple actors under time constraints, where delay erodes commitments and reduces the probability of success. They also recognized the extent to which implementation shapes policy and plans even as it is ostensibly shaped by policy. What people set out to do is often changed by what they are subsequently able to do. Once again, we are reminded of the inseparability of planning and implementation. That said, still missing was any sense of how planners might obtain the power and influence to control commitments and keep the process moving forward.

More recently, a way has been proposed for thinking about implementation that avoids "the hegemonic political discourse" of governance that centers on "ruling through control and steering" (Pløger 2004, 79). It appears under two headings: self-organization and tactical urbanism. Admittedly this is a small niche in the planning theory literature, but it reflects a long-term interest in non-state forms of planning and intervention. It does so by presenting implementation as something that can occur without highly centralized and oftentimes state-based policies and plans. These theorists reject such an approach. Much of the city, they point out, is not planned (at least in a top-down sense) but rather emerges from an array of interdependent actions: "cities are more the product of self-organization and evolutionary processes than of grand design" (Levy, Martens, and van der Heijden 2016, 332).[2] Attention is thus turned away from state plans and projects to civic and popular initiatives that are more or less independent of governments (Rauws 2016). Such initiatives are relatively uncoordinated, spontaneous eruptions of individual actions that produce collective effects, much as might occur with the formation of an informal settlement or the movement of artists into a formerly industrial area. These other collective actions happen in the interstices of the planned city and are as much a part of and essential to the city as the efforts of city governments and developers to fill waterfronts with parks and luxury housing. To state the obvious, such civic initiatives do not need to be implemented in the sense of requiring a central locus of control. Planners do not have to bother themselves with how to initiate them and see them through to completion. For planners, effectiveness is simply not at stake. Nonetheless, it is almost always the case that these developments need to be monitored and regulated in order to mitigate any threats that they might pose to the health and well-being of the city's residents.

Tactical urbanism builds on this notion of self-organization in a way that recognizes how self-organization can serve more collective concerns (Webb 2018). It encompasses temporary, reversible, and low-cost changes to the city's built environment such as pop-up restaurants, portable playgrounds, temporary performance stages, and emergency homeless shelters. Such interventions are a way of making the city more interesting for the middle class as well as fostering alternative sites for spontaneous activity. The latter points to how tactical urbanism can be used politically. As hypothetical examples, think of an anti-abortion group setting up a counseling booth on a downtown street, or a homeless advocacy group placing a pop-up food kitchen in a public park.

Regarding implementation, tactical urbanism significantly reduces it as a problem. Nothing is big and permanent and much of what is done can be left to activist groups around the city. It does not eliminate implementation to the extent that self-organization promises to do. Rather, it suggests that planners think in terms of creating the conditions within which tactical urbanism can happen, for example by ensuring that all neighborhoods have small parks and plazas available for "pop-up" events. Relatedly, planners should develop projects that signal to people that they should recycle their plastic waste, spend more time in public spaces, or take mass transit (or bike) instead of driving their car to and from work. Instead of thinking about coercive measures for encouraging this behavior, planners need to think in terms of subtle cues, for example planting trees in a selected number of parking spaces in the downtown to make it shadier and more pedestrian-friendly and to discourage automobile usage. This is less a matter of implementing a multifunctional plan or large-scale project and more a matter of suggesting small and simple changes that give rise to big consequences.

I suspect that no planning theorist believes that cities can work well and achieve acceptable levels of livability solely on the basis of self-organization and tactical urbanism. State-directed planning and its attention to collective interests is unavoidable, and this makes the problem of implementation unavoidable as well. Once again, the discussion returns to two nagging issues: power and control.

Consider power: planning theorists readily acknowledge that differences in power among groups have a significant impact on the advice that is given and whether or not it is subsequently implemented. Power is conceptualized as a resource (much like wealth or land) that can be deployed to achieve the ends of those who hold it, rather than an outcome of social processes (Metzger, Soneryd, and Hallström 2017). Consequently, the ultimate aim is to amass power. Until then, planners have to take power differentials into account as they go about their work. Such differences create unavoidable conflicts and this means recognizing that planning is, at its roots, a contentious activity (Gualini 2015). As the Norwegian planning scholar John Pløger (2004, 83) has pointed out, planners are frequently faced with "an obstinate, and maybe recalcitrant, public" that creates conflicts that bind them to these publics and with those for whom they work. To plan is to make choices that establish allegiances among different interests and groups and destabilize or reinforce differences in power, resources, opportunities, and even status. Issues of power are intrinsic to planning. The question is what planners should do in response.

The theorist Ernest Alexander (2001), a former U.S. professor of planning and currently practicing in Israel, agreed that, as regards executing, power is the issue. If planners want to be effective, he proposed, they must engage in strategic rationality, that is, the *realpolitik* that Bent Flyvbjerg seemed to reject in his book on rationality and power.[3] Planners should do whatever it takes – within limits, of course, but what limits? – to achieve their goals. Alexander builds his case on the claim that differences create interdependencies and interdependencies create conflicts. Conflicts, moreover, can only be resolved by acting strategically. Communicative engagement, collaboration, and pragmatic sensitivity – because they rely heavily on the reasonableness of people, transparency, and a concern for the common good – are each in their own way problematic in political settings. Planners have to be strategic in order to be effective. Alexander further pointed out that this meant attending to "coercive power, and actors pursuing their own self-interested goals" (p. 317). As should be obvious, this poses significant challenges for planners. Are they to abandon their commitment to the public and act in their self-interest? Are they to be – do they have the power to be – coercive, and do they have the resources and legitimacy to withstand controversy? The U.S. political scholar Alan Altshuler (1965, 356) argued that planners should avoid conflict: "The planner who stirs controversy risks failure." By engaging in controversy, planners risk losing political support and tarnishing their cloak of objectivity. In response to these concerns, Alexander distinguishes between good planning and effective planning. The former involves collaboration alongside truthful and sincere communication in search of consensus; the latter requires engaging in the strategic realities of power. He is silent as to what the latter engagement might entail.

Unlike Alexander, John Forester (2009) remains committed to communicative rationality and is less willing to take up strategic rationality. Democratic deliberations can work, he maintains, even in the presence of power differentials. They do so by judiciously setting in motion facilitating, moderating, and mediating efforts that then enable dialogue, debate, and negotiation to occur. Using such skills, planners can generate alternatives and craft compromises that allow the interests of all parties to be recognized and accommodated. In effect, power is dissolved in the joint search for actions from which all can benefit. In Forester's terms, this is what it means to engage politically. The criticism, of course, is that Forester seems to assume either that all people are reasonable or that those who are unreasonable can be convinced to act otherwise. These are problematic assumptions for those who view the world as replete with deeply rooted contradictions and conflicts.

Most planning theorists believe that planners should engage with power by learning how it is exercised and then incorporating those understandings into what needs to be done. Forester (2011), Margo Huxley (2000) from the United Kingdom, and Charles Hoch (1992) all bring power into planning as something that has to be studied and accounted for when devising plans and advice. This is hardly equivalent to acting in a strategically political fashion. Yet, in a brief commentary in 2011, Forester held out the promise of directly engaging power when he noted that one of "planning's dirty little secrets" is that "someone has to do the work" (p. 326). This could be read as saying that someone has to execute what planners have proposed; someone has to make sure that things get done. The next step in the argument would be to stipulate what that work entails. Instead, Forester advises planners to look for "innovative, creative, and exemplary cases [of good planning] and learn[ing] from them," that is, discover "how good work in messy and tragic circumstances can nevertheless exist" (p. 327). This approach resonates with what Hoch (1984b, 86), a U.S. planning theorist, calls the "mainstream orientation [that] treat[s] power as the capacity of individuals to learn from experience."

Quite interestingly, as regards the political status of planners, Hoch, in his 1992 article cited above, wrote that planners should "grasp the ironic contingency of their work to find support in a solidarity based on the power of shared vulnerability rather than the possession of power" (p. 214). This seems quite unequivocal: planners should acknowledge power but not pursue or exercise it, clearly a cautious approach. The statement also draws what seems to be a questionable moral equivalence between planners and oppressed and marginalized groups, with both subsumed within the same category. Admittedly, it could be read differently, that is, as an implicit suggestion to form coalitions with these groups – alliances among the relatively powerless.

As regards engaging politically and striving to achieve their goals, the overall message being sent by most planning theorists is that planners should engage in "responsible political action" (Hoch 1992, 209). They should not be disruptive or devious, but rather adhere to legitimate forms of political engagement or what the Germany-based theorist Enrico Gualini (2015, 5) labels the "tacit consensus underlying liberal democracy" in which overt conflict is avoided. Though these theorists might acknowledge that power can also be a form of domination, they do not envision planners subjugating others to their will. This aversion to *realpolitik* can also be found – somewhat surprisingly – among those theorists who call for a radical, insurgent planning that empowers marginalized and disadvantaged groups. Yet, here, executing takes a different form.

5.2 Insurgent planning

For radical planning theorists, any social justice achieved from within the state is unlikely to be transformative; at best, it will only marginally improve unjust conditions and certainly not eliminate the forces that give rise to them. After having been helped by the state, marginalized and oppressed people are hardly ever in a better position to act against their oppressors. The issue is "the *reluctance* on the part of planners to provide citizens with real influence regardless of whether they are organized in NGOs or as political activists" (Monno and Khakee 2012, 98, emphasis in original). In part, state planners are blocked from addressing power relations because they are still committed to a modernist planning paradigm that assumes a neutral state, the reachability of consensus, and the viability of an apolitical, technically driven planning (Shrestha and Aranyu 2015, 441). When marginalized and disempowered groups turn to the state for assistance, they run the risk of being coopted into the state's agenda. For significant political transformation to occur, these radical theorists claim, it has to emanate from outside the state and, specifically, in civil society, where people can control the resources that they need to live well. Only then will they be empowered to pursue and defend their interests. Collective action that is bottom-up – emerging from "the grassroots" – is preferred. Civil society has to "organize itself autonomously" if it hopes to avoid cooptation by the state (Lopes de Souza 2006, 328). To be organized by the state or the market and to remain within their sphere is to be constricted to the values and dominant interests of these institutions. Civil society, however, is capable of and "can directly or (pro) actively conceive and, to an extent, implement solutions independently of the state apparatus" (Lopes de Souza 2006, 327). What is therefore required is an insurgent planning independent of the state and the market.[4]

In his intellectual history of planning, Friedmann (1987, 225–308) proposed that planning has roots not only in social reform and the technicalities of policy analysis, but also in oppositional efforts that encompassed utopianism, anarchism, and historical materialism. What these efforts had in common, he wrote, was a critical consciousness that imagined the world as radically different from what it was. This critical spirit was the first step toward social emancipation wherein people could escape the chains of capitalism, the restrictions of state regulations, and societal pressures to conform. This would be followed by collective actions in which oppressed and marginalized people took charge of their destiny by developing alternative ways of living (e.g., cooperative housing, worker-owned firms) or even taking over the state. To engage in insurgent planning, in effect, the planner has to become part of, not just aligned with, alternative and oppositional social movements. And even though insurgent groups have been known to emerge out of and learn from involvement in state-organized initiatives, subsequently acting covertly before severing their ties with the state (Beard 2003), the inclination of insurgent planners is to avoid state-based partnerships.

The mission of insurgent planning is to empower groups who are marginalized and oppressed (Friedmann 1992) by providing them with the resources and skills they need to become autonomous and self-reliant and thus capable of implementing what they have determined needs to be done. It resists the power of the state and of capital and the ideologies they spawn, acts against expectations that powerless groups will not disrupt the status quo, and creates new ways of thinking about, acting within, and living in the world. The last requires a critical historical consciousness that probes the origins of marginalization and imagines alternative futures (Miraftab 2009). Only through resistance and autonomous action can these groups avoid state cooptation. More importantly, in this way alone can society achieve an inclusive democracy, economic growth in which all participate equitably, gender equality, and environmental sustainability. Insurgent planning rests on movement politics and the mobilization of heretofore disempowered people.[5]

To a great extent, and somewhat disappointingly, planning theorists are not very forthcoming about how planners might engage with social movements. Sandercock (1998, 129–159) claimed that popular education and social learning are central to insurgencies and that "[o]n a day-to-day basis, the activity of struggle centres around talk, dialogue, persuasion, negotiation" (p. 158). Her implication is that planners have and can share such skills. That planners have communicative skills and that talk will often touch on technical issues points to additional contributions that planners can make. Even more helpful is Friedmann's (1987, 303–306) fuller rendition of the planner's role. He proposed a list of things that a radical planner can contribute: critiques of the present situation, technical refinement of transformative solutions, general intelligence for strategic initiatives, and knowledge of similar actions that were mounted in the past. These are still very broad tasks, having only a slightly higher specificity than empowerment. Consequently, insurgent planners are left with only general guidance.

Planners are frequently connected to social movements not as political actors marching in protest or organizing sit-ins at governmental buildings, but as experts drawing on their technical and social skills to provide support. Marcuse (2009) calls on insurgent planners to undertake three tasks: expose, propose, and politicize. The first is a form of knowing and, specifically, of uncovering the underlying logics and interests behind the forces that create injustice but are presented as normal. Examples might include the way homes are allocated on the basis of income rather than need or the extent to which mass transit is designed to serve affluent population centers. The second concerns prescription. Here, insurgent planners develop proposals for how to remove unjust conditions and do so while weakening, if not eliminating, the dynamics that give rise to them. The last entails a politicization of their proposals, that is, the identification of the political actions that have to be taken while also providing support for the organizing that has to precede these actions.

More expansively, insurgent planning requires a paradigm shift within the planning profession (Sandercock 1998, 157–159). Communicative action, social learning, and popular education are essential, but these activities already exist within planning. What is different in insurgent planning is that they are set within a consciousness that embraces an epistemology of multiplicities; sensitivity to issues of memory, desire, and spirit; and a cosmopolitan perspective that recognizes the complex and global connectedness of people. So formulated, insurgent planning becomes a place-making, ethical inquiry directed at mobilizing and empowering communities. Paula Meth (2010) from the United Kingdom is even more specific. She calls on insurgent planners to engage with the politics of gender, examine "complex questions of rights, moralities, and rationalism" (p. 248), and situate insurgency in everyday lived relations. Stories have to be told of transformative practices that have been successful at stifling injustice. The thrust of these and other descriptions of insurgent planning is to change how planners think and act with less attention paid to how planners themselves become insurgents. To state it bluntly, what insurgencies need is advocate planners to support and advise them.

The Dutch scholar Justus Uitermark along with his American colleague Walter Nicholls addressed one way of thinking about the connection of planners to insurgent groups (Uitermark and Nicholls 2017). The issue for them was what they labeled the representation dilemma, a relationship that governs the kinds of contributions that planners can make to marginalized communities. The dilemma begins from the premise that state planners have knowledge and skills and an institutional position that place them in a position of relative power. They are privileged. To this extent, they have the potential to be "agents of social justice" (p. 46). But if they represent the interests of marginalized communities to the state and other influential actors, they risk speaking for these communities and taking a position of superiority. The result is the imposition of a privileged conception of social justice and not an understanding built on the everyday experiences of people who are subject to that injustice. But if they become "servants of marginalized communities" (p. 33), channeling the ideas these communities have about social justice, planners stifle their thoughts and voices and jettison any possibility of capitalizing on the privileges they possess, privileges that could benefit marginalized people. They lose their voice and influence. Certainly, more resources and skills would enable marginalized groups to maintain their integrity and diminish any reliance on planners. Until that happens, this representation dilemma has to be managed – it cannot be evaded or erased. Uitermark and Nicholls propose four possible responses to the dilemma, each involving trade-offs. These responses emerge from a two-dimensional typology: one dimension involving engagements with the community (either strong or weak) and the other involving substantive conceptions of justice held by planners (either strong or weak). Traditional, rational planning is weak on both dimensions; it neither strongly engages with marginalized communities nor has a strong sense of social justice. Its opposite is insurgent planning, which entails both a strong engagement and a clear sense of what social justice requires. Collaborative planning is weak from a substantive perspective of social justice and the "just-city" approach distances itself from engagement.

Insurgent planners act within and for social movements and marginalized communities. They work with political activists to document injustice and identify what needs to be done. Their contribution is technical, emotional, and relational but not strategic in a *realpolitik* sense. They are suspicious of the state and enamored by collective and grassroots resistance. Absent from this perspective on insurgent planning, however, is the dissent and even insurgency – rare though it might be – that occurs within the state.

More than a few planners have spoken and acted in opposition to the policies of their agencies. As one example, albeit dated, Needleman and Needleman (1974) documented efforts made in certain U.S. cities in the 1960s and 1970s to facilitate neighborhood planning by designating planning staff to liaise with specific neighborhood groups. A number of these planners were drawn into the worldviews of their assigned neighborhoods and became advocates within the planning agency for neighborhood interests even if those interests exceeded or contradicted what the planning agency was able or wanted to do. They managed the representational dilemma by using their position, knowledge, and skills to align themselves with the neighborhood. This put them in conflict with their superiors. Effectively, they did what they were asked but interpreted it in a way that subverted the interests of the state. The American planners Joel Friedman, Judith Kossy, and Mitt Regan (1980) present another example of insurgency within the state. All were employees of the U.S. Department of Housing and Urban Development at the time they wrote. Their agenda was to work within this state agency to move it toward more progressive policies and programs. For them, this meant advocating for the de-commodification of housing and community development programs in order to sever them from inherently exploitative, market relationships. Additionally, they encouraged progressive planners within governmental agencies to establish and maintain ties with program constituencies, channel information to them, encourage community organizing, and build relationships across bureaucratic boundaries to establish political support for progressive policies.

There have also been instances in the United States in which cities have hired planning directors with progressive credentials (Clavel 1986; Krumholz 1982), who then made social justice or equity guiding principles for how they ran the planning agency. Such hires have almost always required that a progressive political coalition, if not mayor, has been elected to office. Also worth mentioning is that a number of planning professors have become elected officials and, in this position, have advocated for better planning. James Throgmorton, formerly professor of planning at the University of Iowa (U.S.A.), not only sat on a city council but also became the city's mayor and has written extensively on his efforts to foster an inclusive democracy and pursue social justice and sustainability (Throgmorton 2000). Even though these efforts fall well short of what a radical planning theorist might consider insurgency, they nonetheless bring progressive values to state policymaking and make planning more consequential than it would have been otherwise. Much like insurgent planners, these planning activists often reject the modernist assumption of state-based consensus and slip beyond planning's semantic limits.

Although all these insurgent theorists are committed to bringing power and politics to the center of planning practice, they find it difficult to stray beyond planning's communicative and knowledge-based limits. Essentially, they leave its social and technical inclinations intact. Most prominent is their reluctance to cast planners as wholly political actors engaged in *realpolitik*. Much like their non-insurgent counterparts, they are disinclined to engage in implementation. Escape from the centripetal pull of planning's intellectual core seems impossible. Once again, the issue reduces to that of power and how to gather and exercise it.

5.3   Assembling coalitions

For decades, planning theorists have argued that collaboration is the key for planning to be considered legitimate, attuned to local knowledge, and attractive to the kind of political support that contributes to the adoption and implementation of its ideas. Acting with others is essential to both performance and being democratic. Collaboration also speaks to the executing of plans and proposals. If a comprehensive land-use plan is to be implemented and if a development proposal is to avoid debilitating opposition, they need more than the support of the planning agency and the planning commission; they need other allies as well. Public planners are not a powerful group. Insurgent planners who have aligned with oppositional groups also need allies. These groups are usually marginalized and powerless and, acting alone, can hardly realize their objectives. In all these instances, planners need to be part of coalitions. Coalitions bring together resources and influence and have the potential to be stronger politically than any of their members.

As regards governmental planners, the idea is to develop good relationships with other city agencies, council members, and the chief executive (Flyvbjerg 1998). These relationships then need to be augmented with ties to various neighborhood, tax policy, transportation, housing, and environmental groups whose support can be nurtured for projects that serve their interests (Krumholz 1982). Relationships between and coordination among these groups are essential for the implementation of even the simplest of projects (Alexander 1998). Limiting the behavior of planners is the self-imposed stricture against the strategic wielding of power. Public planners are averse to being seen as acting politically and in their self-interest. This might be one reason why theorists are enamored with collaboration (a seemingly apolitical act) but relatively silent as regards coalition-building.

This is not the case for insurgent planners. Friedmann (1987, 400–401) is quite explicit about the need for radical planners to establish informal networks and mobilize political constituents. At issue for him and others on the Left is not just specific struggles – blocking a single project likely to disrupt the neighborhood, passage of legislation that ensures a right to housing, compelling the municipality to deliver water services – but a "restructuring of the basic relations of power" (p. 400). To this extent, movements involving insurgent planning have to be linked to other radical and progressive groups. Each of their initiatives, additionally, should be part of and contribute to an expansive political strategy aimed at bringing about a new social order. Coalitions broaden the planner's perspective and the core issue becomes not the execution of a single initiative but the transformation of society, thereby returning planners to their earlier, utopian and comprehensive aspirations.

Of the planning theorists, the socio-materialists are the most attentive to coalitions or what they term assemblages (Beauregard 2012a; Rydin and Tate 2016). An assemblage, as previously noted, is a network of actors – humans and non-humans – that have come together around a common concern. It might be an assemblage organized around waterfront development that includes environmental advocates, community-based groups from nearby neighborhoods, the city's parks department, local councilors, city planners, newspaper editors, adjacent property owners, and sports and recreation associations. Such an assemblage would also contain non-human things: the land itself, the river, the vegetation on the site, abutting roadways, wildlife, drainage infrastructure, laws governing public land, and maintenance practices. All these entities need to be brought together to create a well-focused coalition that can argue successfully for the project and ensure its implementation. The broader the support and the more actors that are involved, the more likely it is that the new waterfront will be built. In multi-interest, democratic societies, execution is fruitless without an assemblage.

If the assemblage is to be successful at what it does, the planner has to attend to two tasks: achieving stability for the assemblage and delegating responsibilities. For socio-materialist theorists what matters is stability, not change (Beauregard and Lieto 2016). Change is ubiquitous, but projects are only realized when actors are brought into relatively stable configurations. This involves managing the ebb and flow of actors into and out of the assemblage as conditions change and goals are modified. (This task is similar to Pressman and Wildavsky's (1973) concern with maintaining commitment in the face of the unavoidable delays.) Planners also have to recognize that the composition of the assemblage has a direct effect on its performance and the goals being pursued, while the task of the planners is to ensure that what the assemblage initially set out to do is more or less accomplished. The assemblage has to be stable enough to allow this to happen. Stabilizing assemblages also allows planners to act into the future (beyond the present in which the initiative was adopted) and across the jurisdiction for which they are responsible (i.e., beyond the offices of the planning agency). It allows the planner to act at a distance. Assemblages are stabilized coalitions and, once stabilized, able to resist threats to their agendas and to their performance.

Acting at a distance also occurs through delegation. Any assemblage, any coalition, any project involving more than a few individuals, requires a division of labor. Responsibilities have to be distributed among those involved; they have to be assigned to specific actors, with delegation occurring among humans and among humans and non-humans. For example, planners might delegate to the city's environmental agency the task of remediating a toxic site so that it can be rebuilt as a playground. Or they might propose to the parks department that a berm be constructed along the edge of a low-lying area to prevent flooding during the rainy season. The parks department is delegated the task of building the berm and the berm is delegated the task of holding back the water. Delegation to non-human things enables planning to be executed when planners are not there. Planners act at a distance by assigning actions as well as responsibility to things that have more permanence, that is, that are unlikely to move to another job or city, or retire. Heterogeneous actors are brought together – enrolled – in an assemblage that forms around a common project. This shifts the focus of execution from planners collaborating with other humans to humans collaborating with non-humans, and to delegating to both.

This is execution from a different perspective than that proposed by theorists concerned with plan implementation or insurgent planning. Thinking in socio-materialist terms is nonetheless compatible with those approaches. Those concerned with the factors that lead to planning success, for example, note the quality of the plan, with reference primarily to the ideas within it. This concern can be extended to how these ideas are presented in images and text and the physical form of the text itself. Is the plan a large, unwieldy document or a more physically inviting object? Material things matter. Implementation, dependent as it is on a project's scale and complexity, requires not only assemblage-like coordination but the involvement of such non-human elements as scheduling charts. Lastly, insurgent planning too can be framed in this way. Although primarily interested in empowerment and self-reliance, it is also concerned (as is all of planning) with the conditions in which people are living and thus with the material world. Political action is replete with objects from bodies marching in the streets, protest signs, street barricades, and bullhorns to signed agreements. Moreover, it requires coalitions without which the power to make things happen remains out of reach. In brief, within planning, assemblages are as ubiquitous as collaborations.

5.4 Conclusion

To ensure that their plans are realized, to increase the likelihood that their advice will result in material improvements, and to be able to claim that they have been effective, planners need to break through the semantic limits of planning and become involved in the processes whereby proposals become reality. That process is "executing" and it is a political process. By entering it, planners risk losing the legitimacy they have attained through their technical knowledge, analytical skills, and purported objectivity as well as their commitment to the public interest. To engage in a strategically political way, though, is problematic. How much *realpolitik* is too much such that it leaves the core idea of planning in shards? In addressing both state-based implementation and non-state-based insurgent planning, theorists have stopped short of proposing that planners commit to being solely political or even partisan political actors. If they engage in persuasion, they should stay close to the evidence. If they become involved in implementation, they should focus on technical and organizational problems and formal remedies. If engaged in insurgent planning, they should provide support to those who march in the streets, picket city hall, disrupt public meetings, and boycott corporations. No matter what planners do, however, they never act alone.

NOTES

1 As a contrast, Musser (1980, 39) asserts that, as regards planning, "the fundamental limit ... is, of course, the presumption of reasonableness of others."

2 This is also a theme of complexity theory approaches to planning (Batty and Marshall 2009).

3 Uitermark and Nicholls (2017, 34) also call for a *realpolitik* of planning, not for the purpose of effectiveness but for the purpose of social justice. Flyvbjerg's argument regarding power is discussed in Chapters 2 and 4.

4 Friedmann (1992, 7 and 35) contrarily proposed that a strong state, and we might assume that he means a strong progressive or at least democratic state, can contribute to the empowerment of marginalized peoples.

5 A tendency exists to romanticize social movements. By contrast, the Brazilian scholar Marcelo Lopes de Souza (2006, 338) reminds us that planning is neither conservative nor progressive and can be used to oppress as well as liberate. Meth (2010) also points out that insurgent groups are not averse, in some instances, to violence and vigilantism and that resistance can be both liberating and subordinating (e.g., when collective struggles are male dominated).

6 Conclusion

Planning theorists are trapped between two opposing forces. On the one side is the centrifugal draw of planning as an idea. On the other is the centripetal pull of its practice. As an idea, planning conveys a loosely defined attitude to acting in the world with an applicability that is seemingly boundless: the setting aside of capital for investing in a small business, the spacing of one's offspring, the development of a missile defense system, the distribution of population growth across a country's towns, cities, and rural areas. It also holds out the promise of a planned society – the idea writ large – that provides guidance for a broad range of human affairs. In contrast, the practice consists of the various tasks engaged in by those who claim urban and regional planning as a profession. Vacant sites have to be mapped, public meetings held, development regulations adjudicated, and testimony given before the local council. The ties of practice are tenuous, though, and theorists struggle to maintain their focus on the practical when the utopian beckons. They vacillate between their aspirations for order, justice, and democracy and their entanglement in professional and educational obligations.

This nagging tension between an expansive and the constricted sense of planning, between the universal and the particular, haunts planning theory. Consequently, it pervades the four core tasks of knowing, engaging, prescribing, and executing. Theorists encourage planners to respect different types of knowledge and the forms in which each is conveyed, thereby capturing society in its fullness, with knowledge co-produced "on the ground." Deeply important to planners is that purposive action emerges from carefully considered and context-specific knowledge. Knowledge and action are inseparable. At the same time, theorists urge planners to attend to the ubiquitous role of power in making knowledge applicable while remaining vigilant to the ability of the powerful to erase knowledge altogether from consideration. Power looms over planning as a seeming force of nature. In response, theorists aspire to a knowledge wedded to democratic practices. Yet, planners (and their theorists) are reluctant to abandon expertise. No matter how much storytelling occurs, and despite an awareness of knowledge's political nature, planners are still strongly attached to the technical aspects of their work. It matters to planners that what is done makes sense from a perspective rooted in a scientific understanding of how cities and their governments function. Planners can neither escape the particularities of knowledge nor the presence and pressure of concentrated power.

A similar tension pervades engaging. Here lies the pull of democracy and of a planning that is not only democratic in its procedures but sustains that democracy by empowering heretofore marginalized and oppressed groups. Nonetheless, much of planning practice consists of explaining planning proposals to neighborhood groups and meeting with individuals to determine, for example, how much off-street parking can be accommodated on a site or how to achieve the maximum number of housing units given the prevailing development controls. Democracy seems less applicable in these settings. What matters is honest and respectful communication and a commitment to finding a resolution that is agreeable to all parties. Not all that planners need to do, alone or with others, requires being democratic, a distinction many planning theorists consider to be fraught with difficulties. Collaboration and other participatory moments, in which all voices and the knowledge they convey are equally valid, bring democracy back into the discussion. Democracy is of more marginal concern when planners engage with non-human things such as mapping software and wetlands. Here, collaboration takes on a different meaning. Still, is not the inclusion of non-humans itself a democracy of things? Once again, democracy beckons and actions restrain.

Prescribing is also caught in this tension between the upward pull of justice and morality and the downward pull of existing politics and ideologies, let alone the desire actually to do something and be effective. What needs to be done is only an imperfect guide to what ought to be done and what ought to be done has to fit into the realm of what can be done. Where should planners look for guidance on how to negotiate this terrain? Technical understandings, ethical precepts, political affiliations, and ideological dispositions are all, singularly and intertwined, possibilities. These are strategic choices, however, and planners want to act – can only act – at the level of tactics. Frustrating them is that the gap between strategy and tactics is not easily bridged. A planner's Marxist inclinations might point to housing as a right to be placed beyond the commodification imposed by capitalist markets, but proposing that all housing be provided by the state or collectively owned is far from a feasible prescription. For planning to be realized, the motivation of big ideas needs to be grafted onto the messiness of practical and political judgments.

Lastly, consider the core task of executing. Here, the tension between the universal and the particular manifests in two different ways. The first is the semantic limitations of an idea of planning that distinguishes it from action. Yet, to plan and then to distance oneself from the implementation of that plan seems irresponsible not to mention unfulfilling. Planning should be extended beyond this limit. Nevertheless, to travel this path confronts another limitation – planning's aversion to a politics that erodes its technical contribution. To accomplish what has been proposed requires engaging in a power-infused politics that entails more than facts and honest communication. Acting strategically threatens the legitimacy that planners have fought to build and maintain. The tension materializes in a second way as planners recognize that imbalances of power cannot be ignored in realizing the goals of planning. Activism calls. For the more radical of theorists, insurgent planning offers a way to counteract the conservative tendencies of states and markets. Yet, planning activists working within the realm of the state and those acting in opposition still find themselves drawn back to the core of planning and its reluctance to abandon the technical understandings of substance and process that distinguish planners from the many others engaged in changing the world.

Joining these centrifugal and centripetal forces are two other, continually perplexing puzzles with which planning theorists grapple. One has to do with the relationship between theory and practice, or, more precisely, the passage of the academic form of planning theory into the realm of practitioners. If theory fails to negotiate this gap, it remains solely as scholarship, valuable in its own right but nonetheless professionally incomplete. The other concerns planning's role in liberal, capitalist democracies and, specifically, its awkward positioning between the state, the market, and civil society. Planning theorists often portray state planners as relatively autonomous within the state, rather than wholly subservient to it, and able to mediate between the state and non-state actors. Whether accurate or not, this is a highly unstable situation. The discussion of both of these issues will lead me to reflect briefly on the future of planning theory and of urban and regional planning itself.

6.1   Theory and practice

More than a few planning theorists have noted a gap between their theoretical insights and the adoption of those insights by practitioners (Alexander 2010; Dyckman 1983, 5; Innes 1995). This slippage between theory and practice is to be expected: the abstractions of the former are not meant to and can never equate perfectly to the concrete particularities of the latter. Given the pressures on academics to train practitioners and for their work to be relevant to the profession, though, academic theorists cannot help but ask to what extent the ideas they profess make their way to and influence the planning that is done. To this extent, the objective of theory – always a normative task – is not simply to interpret planning practice but to guide it as well. To this extent, such a stance implies that theory is produced outside of practice and then added to it, as if practitioners themselves were incapable of thinking theoretically. It is widely recognized that many planners do reflect on what they do and learn from experience. They are guided by reflection-in-action (Schön 1982) and, from a certain perspective, have no need to draw upon academic theories.[1]

If practitioners develop theory out of their experiences, then what is the purpose of academic theory (beyond the profession's scholarly legitimacy) and what is its relation to practice? Except for a few Marxist-based scholars, almost all theorists would reject the assertion that theory is what drives social change; that is, that people institute reforms when a theory convinces them to do so. Still, Dyckman (1969), in one of the earliest statements on the utility of planning theory, argued that its purpose was to provide practitioners with justification for their actions. In effect, theory legitimates practice. More broadly embraced is that when theory is built on and out of practice, it gives everyone a better understanding of what they are doing (Binder 2011). As Susan Fainstein wrote with her U.S. colleague Scott Campbell (Fainstein and Campbell 2012, 3), the point of planning theory is to "enable practitioners to achieve a deeper understanding of the processes in which they are engaged than can be attained through simple intuition or common sense." The value being espoused is critical reflection, an objective that nonetheless leaves undefined any specific theoretical approach. It is assumed that out of critical reflection grows a "better" planning.

Regardless of whether theory is intended to motivate, guide, or enlighten, most of the debate about closing the theory–practice gap focuses on which approach best fits planning practice. This became quite explicit when, in the 1990s, "armchair" theorists – the reference being to the Marxists and postmodernists – were criticized by Judith Innes for developing perspectives so distant from planning practice as to be of little relevance (Innes 1995). Communicative planning and collaborative planning theory were proposed to narrow the theory–practice gap by building theory on what planners actually do in their daily practice (Forester 2009). This would make it possible for theorists to "pursue the questions and puzzles that arise" (Innes 1995, 183) in practice leading eventually to emancipatory knowledge. Planning theory had to be situated; it had to be context dependent (Watson 2008, 224). Innes and Booher (2010) went even further and found ways to apply their approach to real-world situations and engage directly in practice. Claiming that forming social relationships and talking with others was essential for effective planning, they developed ideas which, they believed, would help planners to do this. Theory would encourage practitioners to think about how to plan. It would guide them in their practical judgements of what to do when and with whom.

The U.K. planning scholar Alex Lord (2013) has rejected approaches to planning practice that privilege "the primacy of testimony" (p. 28). He sees talk as reifying intersubjectivity and, contrary to what communicative practice and collaboration theorists claim, decontextualizing planning. Nevertheless, Lord believes that language is the correct starting point for planning theory. His problem is with the impulse to theorize, that is, to explain and attempt to guide practice. For him, theory needs to be less "theoretical" and more "investigative" (p. 32). It should think in terms of Wittgensteinian language games, with the theorist's attention directed at the strategic moves of practitioners, the way meaning is constituted, and how language and action are linked. Planning theory becomes useful to the extent that it reveals how practice is done in specific, contextualized, linguistic encounters. Only by becoming non-theoretical – in the sense of reflecting back to practitioners what they have done – can theory be convincing to those who might use it. Theory is not meant to change practice. In this sense, Lord's criticism seems more directed at critical theory than theory itself.

Lord's argument is a reaction to the phenomenological approach of people like the American theorist Richard Bolan (1980). Bolan suggested that the theory–practice gap could be closed if theorists acknowledged that planning is always specific and concrete and done in situations that are always both relatively unique and inherently ambiguous. The object of planning theory should be the planning episode, that is, a specific situation in which the practitioner encounters the world in its totality, with each episode significantly different from the others. So immersed, the practitioner draws on prior experiences and her sense of existing circumstances to develop an understanding of the situation and of the best way to behave within it. Knowledge derives from action and the planner is "ultimately the theorist for any given planning episode" (p. 271). The implication, of course, is that no need exists for a theory to be imported into the planning episode: "there is no place for the luxury of abstraction or compartmentalization of experience and knowledge" (p. 271). This seems a rejection of theory itself. Yet, in developing his argument, Bolan deploys elaborate diagrams to present the multitude of factors that characterize any planning episode. His analytical presentation thus signals the need for theoretical reflection and the relevance of scholars like himself. Practitioners might be their own theorists, but the implication is that academic theorists are still needed.

Similar to what Lord proposed, yet not fully embracing it, the Italian planning theorist Stefano Moroni (2010b) makes a partial retreat from the possibility of using theory to guide action. Moroni, though, still believes in theory. As he sees it, the problem is which theory is best tailored to practice and, more specifically, which kind of practice. In effect, the gap can be closed by a meta-theory that enables practitioners to select what theoretical tool to use in which planning situation. That theory influences practice, Moroni claims, is both "obvious and inevitable" (p. 146). The task of the theorist is "to foster critical debate around the theories that inevitably underlie practice" (p. 148). Moroni's specific prescription is to abandon a teleocratic approach to theory that is top-down, directional, and coordinative and based on authoritative rules. Instead, the theorist should commit to a nomocratic approach that recognizes the complexity and unpredictability of cities and the spontaneous order of practice and do so without abandoning the norms of planning. Consequently, he rejects both communicative planning and collaborative approaches because they strive for coordination and thereby stifle the emergence of "advantageous social-spatial spontaneous orders" (p. 146). Moroni proposes instead a nomocratic theory that has the potential to transform practice and, in this way, close the theory–practice gap by bringing practice in line with theory.

Michael Gunder (2010b), a New Zealand planning theorist, has taken a different approach. He has claimed that planning theory does not matter to practitioners because theorists fail to recognize that "under-standing social reality requires an understanding of the human subject" (p. 48). He urges theorists to embrace the psychoanalytical writings of Jacques Lacan. Lacan viewed people as alienated from "the Real" and, in reaction, they are pulled toward symbolic fantasies and ideological illusions that make it difficult to act appropriately. To be in the world, planners have less need of science or theory than of a deeper under-standing of the unconscious motivational desires involved in planning practice. Practice is the sum of individual desires, with self-knowledge enabling the planner to realize his expertise. Essentially, the theory–practice gap is a consequence of theory not matching what practice actually entails, or, more precisely, the psychological predispositions of the people who plan.

For other theorists, the problem is the tendency of planning theorists to lodge their arguments in a critical theory that is moral and political rather than addressed to the substantive conditions confronting prac-titioners (March 2010). Two Australian scholars, Tony Sorensen and Martin Auster (1999), are quite explicit about this. In their review of Leonie Sandercock's book *Towards Cosmopolis*, a book that proposed a critical, multicultural, and progressive approach to planning theory, they accused her of being an incurable romantic whose understand-ing of planning and the profession is "excessively broad" (p. 148) and which wholly misses the fact that "perhaps 80 to 90 percent of practic-ing planners' time" (p. 147) is spent addressing the unavoidable restric-tions within development controls. In effect, what planners essentially do is deal with mundane, if nonetheless consequential, matters. They are not asked to make "critical" choices. Embracing critical theory would put planners on the fringes of society and so marginalize them as to make them incapable of earning a living. Sorensen and Auster point out that the profession cannot afford to be politically conten-tious. Consequently, the gap between theory and practice continues to increase as theorists stay cloistered in their world of critical theory and statutory planning loses touch with its reformist history while becoming ever more market based.

In their critique, Sorensen and Auster also note the normative as well as utopian tendencies of planning theory and the latter's stark contrast with the practicalities of actual planning. To an extent, the evidence supports their accusation. Numerous planning scholars have observed that it is almost impossible to find a planning episode that was guided by a specific academic theory. Examining three instances in Australia,

Alan March (2010) noted that planners will use theory when it serves to justify a project or a way of approaching it, that is, when circumstances allow. Otherwise, theory is absent. What matters more than theory is the institutional framework in which planners work. Practitioners are enmeshed in already-established laws and regulations, bureaucratic procedures, political relationships, and precedents. This is what draws their attention and guides their actions. They plan by adapting to the constrains that confront them.

This perspective resonates with Ernest Alexander's (2010) claim that the theory–practice gap is less an issue of translation in which a theory enters into practice and is adapted to the specific situation and more an issue of enlightenment. Theory filters into practice primarily through professional education but also through electronic and print media, conferences, and public meetings. Students are exposed to different normative arguments and procedural possibilities and this instills in them aspirations useful in future employment. In this fashion, theory "informs 'good' practice by 'enlightening' practitioners to improve their judgment, rather than equipping them with technologies for better practice" (Alexander 2010, 100). Of course, March's point – that theory is only used when circumstances allow – now becomes relevant in that these aspirations can easily fall victim to the pressure of institutional arrangements that planners can neither change nor violate with impunity.

Many of these theorists seem to be suggesting that planning (aside from its technical understandings of urban and regional development) is basically common sense; that is, it requires people who are able to grasp the imperatives of a situation and act accordingly. Essentially, good planners are simply good pragmatists in a practical rather than philosophical sense. Bent Flyvbjerg (2001) pointed in this direction when he called for planners to accept that scientific procedures and technical knowledge were less important than practical wisdom, what in Greek is known as *phronesis*. Science (*episteme*) and technique (*techne*), he offered, have turned planning scholars toward the epistemology of the natural sciences and blinded them to the contingent and reflexive nature of social relations. Universalizing logics make no sense in the world of planning. Required instead is an understanding of possibilities, ambiguities, and uncertainties in specific contexts. And, because it is planning, attention has to be given to moral choices and consequences as well. Planning theory should "contribute to society's practical rationality in elucidating where we are, where we want to

go, and what is desirable according to diverse sets of values and interests" (p. 167). The Australian planning scholar Jean Hillier (1995) is
of a similar mind as regards the centrality of *phronesis* to planning
practice. Like Flyvbjerg, she resists the reduction of common sense
to simply intuition, but nonetheless retains the centrality of practical
wisdom and the flexibility and sensibility that it implies. Consequently,
planning theories need to "ask pragmatic questions concerning appropriate strategies which may help to satisfy people's contingent needs
and desires and ethical questions about the issue of developing plans
for the public good in the light of socioculturally conditioned self-
interpretations and knowledge" (Hillier 1995, 295).

For many planning theorists, the theory–practice gap can be closed by
moving theory closer to – or even merging it with – the particularistic
rhythms of practice while retaining a moral sensibility and a political
awareness. Even if theory were to better mimic practice, and manage
to do so critically, the question still remains whether it can be so useful
and compelling as to guide what practitioners do, that is, for them to
commit to a specific theoretical approach. The prospects do not look
promising. The specificity of actual events and the persistent problem
of translation from theory to practice seem insurmountable. It might
well be that theorists will have to settle for Alexander's second option:
influencing practice through enlightening students.

Lurking within this story are ominous signs that planning theory itself
might be in trouble. If theorists are unable to close the theory–practice
gap, does this not leave planning theory and those who write and teach
it vulnerable to irrelevance? Marginal to practice, theory becomes marginal to professional education as well. In fact, planning theory might
have been most welcomed institutionally – that is, most respected –
during the late 1950s and 1960s when postwar urban growth propelled
municipalities to hire planners and universities to mount and expand
planning programs.[2] Planning theory provided university-based
planning education with legitimacy; it served as an intellectual and
scholarly equivalent to social science (Beauregard 2015, 192–210) on
the one hand and to architectural theories on the other. During these
years, it also benefitted from the aura of "grand theory" that characterized then-current scholarship (Bolan 1980). Theory, in its formal
sense, had academic value. And, since the planning profession was
then enthralled by technology and the power of governments to act
for the common good (a legacy of World War II), rational approaches
to practice were still in vogue. This attitude supported corresponding

theories which placed planners at the center of public initiatives. Today, planning programs no longer need intellectual credentials to survive (the university itself having become more professionalized), the social sciences are no longer (with exceptions) dominated by grand theory, and the government is no longer revered as the solution to the social ills that beset cities and regions.

In fact, there has never been a groundswell of enthusiasm for planning theory within the profession. In the United States, planning theory is not (and has hardly ever been) a major aspect of planning education even though it seems always to be present; for example, programs rarely hire someone just to teach theory, but theory is almost always taught in some fashion. And while the professional association expects planners to be exposed to planning theory, it is a very minor part of what it asks of planning education. Further evidence for this gloomy view is that there seem to be fewer major figures in planning theory whose ideas dominate the debates and whom other theorists feel it necessary to read, or who make planning theory compelling within planning education. In its "golden age" from the 1960s through to the 1990s, people like John Friedmann, Susan Fainstein, Patsy Healey, John Forester, and Andreas Faludi rose to prominence and anchored the theoretical project. Today, being a theorist and only a theorist is not a promising career plan for a young planning scholar. This is not to say that planning theory will soon no longer be taught or that scholars will no longer write books and articles on planning theory, but rather to point out its professional marginality despite its intellectual significance. That said, a number of scholars have made a career in planning theory and continue the planning theory project in important ways: Heather Campbell, Stefano Moroni, Jean Hillier, Michael Gunder, and Ernest Alexander come quickly to mind. The "big" names, however, have retired or are much less active; these others, moreover, are mostly mid-career and not newly minted scholars. That said, particularly given the employment prospects for planning theorists, the future looks bleak.

Intellectual perspectives do not last forever; they are not eternal. No formally framed planning theory existed in the early 20th century and one can assume that a time will come when it ceases to be written. This is not a matter of intellectual fashion but rather of the changing nature of social practices and institutional supports. I suspect, though, that most if not all planning theorists (myself included) find planning theory's demise impossible to imagine. Does this mean that people will act without reflection? Will large projects and cities not need to be coordinated and their activities organized? Is the implication that reflection-in-practice will become so accepted in the field that no one will see any value in writing about it? Or, will the denouement come from planners moving away from the claim to be professionals and instead reimagine planning as a craft to be learned, as it once was, "on the job"? If planning is truly a matter of practical wisdom, maybe it is best absorbed experientially rather than in the classroom or by reading books such as this one.

Countervailing forces to the disappearance of planning theory also exist. Many young planning scholars write planning theory, even if it is not their primary interest. Two journals – *Planning Theory* and *Planning Theory and Practice* – are devoted to its writing; other journals willingly accept articles on the topic. Monographs and anthologies are published and purchased. Moreover, planning theory is still taught in planning programs, an indication of a belief that planning theory contributes to the field: if not now providing it with intellectual legitimacy and cachet, at least distinguishing planning from related fields such as urban studies or public administration. As long as practitioners have not become automatons, continue to reflect on what they do, and have influence over it, there will be scholars who are curious and who feel the need not just to publicize these practices but improve them as well. Speaking as a committed theorist, it is inconceivable to me that professional planners might not need to reflect on what they do or that the profession can function without a moral and intellectual conscience. Absent both, planning loses its professional aura.

Arguably the strongest argument for why planning theory will continue to be written, at least in the foreseeable future, is the very unruliness of this endeavor. The observation of two planning scholars a few years back is still accurate in 2020: planning theory "display[s] a remarkably healthy state of (postmodern?) heterogeneity" (Huxley and Yiftachel 2000, 336). The literature contains numerous critiques of the dominant approaches along with a variety of thematic entry-points – strife, forgetting, trust, agonism, obduracy, being – that stray from the purported center and resist the centripetal force of paradigm-building. A variety of ways of thinking theoretically about planning exist, from Foucaultian, Heideggerian, and Lacanian analyses to chaos theory, phenomenology, and actor-network theory. In 2018 (Barry et al. 2018), a group of young scholars in the United States challenged older scholars to unsettle planning theory. Theory, they argued, is always an attempt to root understandings whereas a scholarly discipline advances only when existing viewpoints are upended. Their prescription was to disrupt "the practice of theorizing, the habits of inquiry, interpretation, and relational sense-making" (p. 434) that currently exist. Their specific recommendations, however, did not break far from arguments already existing in the literature: moving planning theory away from process to substantive outcomes and particularistic practices, attending more closely to the voices of vulnerable people, and embracing pragmatism. This should not detract from the very important point that they are making. Nor is it reason to cast aside the possibility and the necessity for planning theory to become, not too long into the future, unrecognizable to its current practitioners. The strength of any intellectual project lies in its diversity and disagreements, not in its consensus.

6.2 The future of planning

Interestingly, planning theorists worry less about the future of their intellectual project than about planning itself. Their anxiety is mainly provoked by the ebb and flow of conservative politics and its opposition to any and all perceived threats to individual freedom or interference in the workings of the free market.[3] One form this anxiety takes is a nostalgia for an idyllic time when planning was not just comprehensive but attentive to social concerns. Then, supposedly, planners were intent on bringing order to an otherwise undisciplined city and addressing the many ills associated with widespread poverty and deprivation. Both concerns, however, seem to have been pushed aside by planning's turn away from social reform (Sorensen and Auster 1999) and by its embrace of economic growth and city competitiveness. The result has been a shift that substitutes narrowly conceived strategic plans and large real-estate development projects for a planning that aspires to organizing the city for the common good (Fainstein 2005b; Taşan-Kok 2012). Project-based planning rules. Real-estate development and such infrastructural projects as light-rail, critics claim, have become the keys to economic growth and dominate local governmental planning. Embracing this approach, governmental planners have been accused of turning away from the living conditions of those in need to those people whose lives are served by office buildings, luxury apartments, and international airports. Consequently, public planning does not serve everyone, but only the few. To this extent, it is no longer planning as it had been historically conceived. It no longer aspires to a reformist version of the public interest. Rather, the common good is defined as economic growth, leaving the distribution of the benefits of that growth to the market.

Behind this swerve from reformist plans to growth-oriented projects is a corresponding shift of local governments from being primarily engaged in service provision to greater emphasis on competitiveness and entrepreneurialism (Beauregard 2015, 172–191; Lovering 2009). Since the 1970s, elected officials have become increasingly fixated on competing with other cities and with their surrounding areas for capital investment and the jobs and tax revenues that such investment promises. They have elevated economic development to a major function of local government and, in doing so, diminished the influence of the city's planning agency. The emphasis is less on managing growth and ensuring that the city provides for all its residents and more on launching initiatives that encourage a particular type of growth. This is done by supporting investors, reducing regulatory restraints, and subordinating planning concerns to the needs of capital. To this extent, it looks to these theorists that certain core concerns of planning – the public interest, acting democratically, acknowledging expertise, being transparent – are being eroded and that planning, as they conceive it, is losing its institutional place within local government to economic development and business interests. A loss so profound could well mean irrelevance.

From its adoption by local governments in the early 20th century to the post-World War II period, planning seemed to have substantial political support and little political opposition. This continued even during the anti-communism of the postwar decades that tethered planning ideologically to totalitarianism. In the United States mainly, but in England as well, one of the great fears was that communism would spread into heretofore democratic societies and result not just in the cessation of individual freedoms but also in the imposition of centralized planning. The economist Friedrich Hayek (1944) in his book *The Road to Serfdom* made this point quite explicitly. He argued that planning could only be effective to the extent to which it extended its control throughout society. To achieve its aims, it had to limit all deviations from the plan and, in doing so, seriously curtail the "autonomous spheres in which the ends of the individual are supreme" (p. 56). To this criticism he added the further claim that in order to assert that control, planners had to have full knowledge of the workings of society, a goal they could never reach. Unable to know everything, they would act according to the preferences of bureaucrats and public officials who themselves were responding to the demands of politically influential groups (Low 1991, 169). All this would be contrary to the way markets work and people behave and lead to a society functioning well short of its potential. In Hayek's world, "planning leads to dictatorship because dictatorship is the most effective instrument of coercion and the enforcement of ideals" (p. 70).

To many planning scholars, Hayek was the anti-planner (Low 1991, 162–187). Yet, Hayek's aversion was not to planning itself but to a national and centralized planning that embodied both collectivism and a planned economy (Lai 1999). Local planning, also known as town planning or land-use planning, did not pose for him similar threats to individual freedom and the proper performance of markets. Hayek opposed proposals for the nationalization of land, rent control, betterment levies, and various town and country planning acts. Yet, he also recognized that land markets were rife with unacknowledged consequences (i.e., negative externalities) that impeded their ability to allocate land according to rational criteria. Property owners were not compelled to take into account the harm done to other people's property when, for example, they located a noxious factory adjacent to a residential area. Consequently, Hayek understood the need for a mechanism to make the market more efficient. Imperfect land markets needed to be corrected and town planning was one possible and acceptable response. He additionally recognized that for social purposes such as building schools, the government would have to engage in compulsory purchase so as to obtain the needed land. As long as this purchase was made at market value, he was satisfied. Hayek, then, was not opposed to planning per se. As he wrote: "we should handle our common problems as rationally as possible and that, in so doing, we should use as much foresight as we can command" (Hayek 1944, 34). Hayek and his fellow libertarians did not pose a threat to local planning, which is mainly what urban and regional planning is about, but to central economic planning.[4]

The early postwar reaction against planning and the communism and socialism to which it could easily be associated did not derail the expansion of city planning and, to that extent, did not concern planning theorists. Theorists focused on the local level of planning not the national level. Planning was more directly threatened by the rise of conservatism in the 1980s (particularly in the United States, Australia, and the United Kingdom) and by the more recent emergence of an anti-state, anti-immigrant, and virulently nationalist populism in numerous countries around the world. This combined with a faltering of the capitalist economy (particularly, the global recession of the mid-1970s and that of 2008) and a decline in national governmental support for localities has pushed municipal governments to be entrepreneurial while, at the same time, requiring them to cut costs by shrinking services. Of little surprise, the services most vulnerable to austerity measures are those such as libraries, playgrounds, public health care, and social housing that serve the city's less affluent and less politically influential populations. Inclusive and socially concerned governmental planning has been curtailed as well. To survive within government, public planning has had to turn to austerity planning, attracting capital, and making the city more competitive, not address injustice.

To this extent, the New Right of the 1980s as it was called then, posed a threat to planning as it had been originally conceived and as it was then practiced (Allmendinger 2009, 105–127; Dyckman 1983; Taylor 1998, 130–154). Entrepreneurialism displaced the welfare state and individualism made collectivism and the common good politically untenable. Keynesian interventionism was rejected. The call rang out loudly for privatizing public services, deregulation, and pro-market development strategies. For solutions to society's problems and future prospects, people were encouraged to look toward the free market. Unrestrained by the heavy hand of government, the market would provide. Citizens would become consumers of public goods and services, just as they did for private goods and services. As had occurred in the early 20th century in a number of countries, the intent was to make government more business-like. Now, it would also be business-friendly. Planners would be asked to serve the market and to manage the downsizing of the public sphere. Planning theorists thus began to consider what it meant to plan not for growth or welfare but for austerity (Burton and Murphy 1980). This collapse of the liberal consensus and the corresponding end of postwar prosperity led to the emergence of Marxist planning theory as critique and of a more interactional procedural planning as resistance (Hague 1991). In the latter case, a more democratic planning, it was hoped, would protect public planning from being further marginalized.

By the early 2000s, this political threat to planning became known as the neoliberal turn and much local planning came to be seen by planning theorists as neoliberal planning (Gleeson and Low 2000). Neoliberalism erased the liberal values that had underpinned planning since its inception: "representative democracy, individual liberties and freedom of expression, modest power-sharing and public participation" (Watson 2006, 37). The market – free, prescient, superior, and unerring – was now the key to prosperity and the arbiter of public decision-making regarding development. Planning had become "primarily the business of providing private interests with public resources" (Lovering 2009, 1), supporting not supplanting the market and, even more pointedly, not interfering in its functioning. The result was a new planning subjectivity in which social justice and citizen well-being were marginalized and competition, growth, and economic calculation took their place (Baeten 2012). In addition, public responsibilities under neoliberal governance were transferred to quasi-governmental bodies and private entities, collective goals and social cohesion were ignored, participatory and democratic processes were bypassed, and planners were reduced to information providers who "recommend[ed] the thresholds of safe behavior to consumer-citizens" (Taşan-Kok 2012, 15). In essence, "the ideas behind neoliberalism ... are hostile to planning" (Allmendinger 2009, 108).

This was not the planning that most planning theorists, liberal to radical in their politics, envisioned. What neoliberalism had done was to produce an "opportunity-driven pseudo-planning" (Lovering 2009, 4). Three U.K. planning theorists were consequently compelled to ask whether there was a space for better planning in a neoliberal world (Campbell, Tait, and Watkins 2014). A "better" planning would produce outcomes "that seek to further the normative ideals of planning" (p. 46). What theorists needed to do, they suggested, was develop procedures for identifying what might have happened in a given planning situation but did not, that is, what choices and options had been available but ignored. The goal would be to provide planners with the means of identifying the various opportunities available to realize better but unconsidered outcomes. In effect, they counseled planners to accept the fact of a neoliberal world, be critical, and look to make good compromises.

Campbell, Tait, and Watkins (2014) thus attempted to rescue planning from insignificance by returning to its reformist roots. What planning can do, and what it needs to do, is make capitalist democracies work better and do so in ways that favor those who are disadvantaged. Planning is still needed. While this is not a strong argument, it is nonetheless indicative of the response planning theorists have had to the threat posed by neoliberalism. On the one hand, they have mounted critiques and proposed radical resistance; on the other hand, they have continued to proselytize for a planning that is more democratic, more just in its outcomes, more attentive to common concerns, and less subservient to market forces. Neoliberalism is not viewed as an existential threat and a step along the path to extinction. Rather, it simply reinforces what theorists believe to be challenges that planners in liberal democracies have always faced. The object to which theory ostensibly refers might be different, but planning has not disappeared and theory is safe.

6.3   Final thoughts

As do many of these theorists, I think planning theory has to engage more directly with the world – and with practice – as it is and as it could be. For me and others (Beauregard 2015; Lieto and Beauregard 2013; Rydin 2014; 2012; Rydin and Tate 2016), this means, in part, taking greater account of material reality. Too much of planning theory treats action as solely a matter of humans interacting with each other and through the various organizations and institutions that they have devised. Almost wholly ignored is that the material world affords – enables and resists – what planners wish to do. Absent its engagement with non-human things from computers to printed documents to conference tables and from paved plazas to sites for social housing, planning does not exist. Planning is not solely a social act but rather an action intricately intertwined with particular places and material objects. And once plans are made, they encounter a material world whose obduracy will have a great deal to say about whether or not planners are successful. In effect, my challenge to planning theorists is to be post-humanists, materialists, and realists and to place themselves within rather than outside the conditions that exist.

Engaging the material world, with all its human complications, however, does not mean abandoning alternative political possibilities and a critical and moral perspective. Planning can always be done differently and should always be judged not on whether it has achieved its self-proclaimed goals but on whether it has been democratic and enhanced democracy, acted justly and reduced injustices, and pushed at and beyond the limits of institutional constraints. Just as theorists at the political center caution restraint, those to their political left are compelled to pull in the opposite direction. Safely ensconced in the university, planning theorists are particularly well positioned to offer critical commentary and propose alternative approaches.

I am under no illusion that this particular package of socio-materiality, critical theory, and Left politics will appreciably reduce the theory–practice gap or prevent planning from being (further) marginalized within government. Neither am I so naïve to believe that other theorists – each with their own obsessions – will be so enlightened by what I have to say that, in response, they will cast aside their interests to embrace what I find to be most fascinating and useful about planning theory. That they might decline to join with me (and others) in this specific theoretical project is merely another sign of the unruliness of the theoretical project. Yet, and despite planning theory's diversity, there is a core, even if this core is unstable and embarrassingly frayed around its edges. The core is a search for how people can act reasonably, responsibly, and collectively to consider and act upon not only the concerns they have in common but the desire to live together in a world that is democratic, just, sustainable, and more equal than it is now.

NOTES

1 Another, related gap, discussed earlier, is that between theories developed in the global North and those appropriate for the global South (Harrison 2006).

2 Intellectually, planning theory was arguably considerably more robust in the 1980s when the currently dominant theories were developed and refined.

3 Planning theorists are also provoked by the Left, but these critics still believe in planning: they just want to make it insurgent.

4 For an argument that rejects the dichotomy of plan and market, see Alexander (2008).

References

Abram, Simone A. (2000). "Planning the Public," *Journal of Planning Education and Research* 19, 4: 351–357.

Alexander, Ernest (2010). "Introduction: Does Planning Theory Affect Practice, and If So, How?" *Planning Theory* 9, 2: 99–107.

Alexander, E.R. (2008). "Between State and Market," *International Planning Studies* 13, 2: 119–132.

Alexander, E.R. (2001). "The Planner-Prince: Interdependence, Rationalities and Post-Communicative Practice," *Planning Theory and Practice* 2, 3: 311–324.

Alexander, E.R. (1998). "Planning and Implementation," *International Planning Studies* 3, 3: 303–320.

Alexander, E.R. and Andreas Faludi (1989). "Planning and Plan Implementation," *Environment and Planning B* 16, 2: 127–140.

Allmendinger, Philip (2009). *Planning Theory.* New York: Palgrave Macmillan.

Allmendinger, Philip (2002a). "Towards a Post-Positivist Typology of Planning Theory," *Planning Theory* 1, 1: 77–99.

Allmendinger, Philip (2002b). *Planning Theory.* New York: Palgrave Macmillan.

Alterman, Rachel (1982). "Implementation Analysis in Urban and Regional Planning," pp. 225–245 in Patsy Healey, Glen McDougall, and Michael T. Thomas, eds, *Planning Theory.* Oxford: Pergamon Press.

Altshuler, Alan (1965). *The City Planning Process.* Ithaca, NY: Cornell University Press.

Archibugi, Franco (2007). *Planning Theory.* Milan: Springer-Verlag Italia.

Arnstein, Sherry (1969). "A Ladder of Citizen Participation," *Journal of the American Institute of Planners* 35, 4: 216–224.

Baer, William C. (1987). "General Plan Evaluation Criteria," *Journal of the American Planning Association* 63, 3: 329–344.

Baeten, Guy (2012). "Neoliberal Planning: Does It Really Exist?" pp. 205–211 in Tuna Taşan-Kok and Guy Baeten, eds, *Contradictions of Neoliberal Planning.* Dordrecht: Springer.

Banfield, Edward (1959). "Ends and Means in Planning," *International Social Science Journal* 11, 3: 361–368.

Barry, Janie, Megan Horst, Andy Inch, et al. (2018). "Unsettling Planning Theory," *Planning Theory* 17, 3: 418–438.

Basta, Claudia (2016). "From Justice *in* Planning toward Planning *for* Justice," *Planning Theory* 15, 2: 190–212.

Batty, Michael and Stephen Marshall (2009). "The Evolution of Cities: Geddes, Abercrombie and the New Physicalism," *Town Planning Review* 80, 6: 551–574.

Beard, Victoria (2003). "Learning Radical Planning," *Planning Theory* 2, 1: 13–35.

Beauregard, Robert A. (Forthcoming). "The Entanglements of Uncertainty," *Journal of Planning Education and Research*.

Beauregard, Robert A. (2015). *Planning Matter: Acting with Things*. Chicago, IL: University of Chicago Press.

Beauregard, Robert A. (2013). "The Neglected Places of Practice," *Planning Theory and Practice* 14, 1: 8–19.

Beauregard, Robert A. (2012a). "In Search of Assemblages," *Crios* 4: 9–16.

Beauregard, Robert A. (2012b). "Planning with Things," *Journal of Planning Education and Research* 32, 2: 132–140.

Beauregard, Robert A. (2002). "New Urbanism: Ambiguous Certainties," *Journal of Architectural and Planning Research* 19, 3: 181–194.

Beauregard, Robert A. (1998). "Subversive Histories: Texts from South Africa," pp. 184–197 in Leonie Sandercock, ed., *Making the Invisible Visible*. Berkeley, CA: University of California Press.

Beauregard, Robert A. (1995). "Challenges to Progressive Service Organizations: Planact of South Africa," *Community Development Journal* 20, 4: 369–371.

Beauregard, Robert A. (1991). "Without a Net: Modernist Planning and the Postmodern Abyss," *Journal of Planning Education and Research* 10, 3: 189–194.

Beauregard, Robert A. and Laura Lieto (2016). "Does Actor Network Theory Help Planners to Think about Change?" pp. 159–174 in Yvonne Rydin and Laura Tate, eds, *Actor Networks of Planning*. London: Routledge.

Beckman, Norman (1964). "The Planner as Bureaucrat," *Journal of the American Institute of Planners* 30, 4: 323–327.

Beebeejaun, Yasminah (2006). "The Participation Trap: The Limitations of Participation for Ethnic and Racial Groups," *International Planning Studies* 11, 1: 3–18.

Benveniste, Guy (1977). *The Politics of Expertise*. San Francisco, CA: Boyd and Fraser.

Binder, Geoffrey (2011). "Theory(izing) Practice: The Model of Recursive Cultural Adaptation," *Planning Theory* 11, 3: 221–241.

Bolan, Richard (1980). "The Practitioner as Theorist: The Phenomenology of the Professional Episode," *Journal of the American Planning Association* 46, 3: 261–274.

Boyer, M. Christine (1983). *Dreaming the Rational City*. Cambridge, MA: The MIT Press.

Burton, Dudley J. and M. Brian Murphy (1980). "Democratic Planning in Austerity," pp. 177–205 in Pierre Clavel, John Forester, and William W. Goldsmith, eds, *Urban and Regional Planning in an Age of Austerity*. New York: Pergamon Press.

Camhis, Marios (1979). *Planning Theory and Philosophy*. London: Tavistock Publications.

Campbell, Heather (2012). "Planning to Change the World," *Journal of Planning Education and Research* 32, 2: 135–146.

Campbell, Heather (2006). "Just Planning: The Art of Situated Ethical Judgment," *Journal of Planning Education and Research* 26, 1: 92–106.

Campbell, Heather (2002). "Planning: An Idea of Value," *Town Planning Review* 73, 3: 271–288.

Campbell, Heather, Malcolm Tait, and Craig Watkins (2014). "Is There Space for Better

Planning in a Neoliberal World?" *Journal of Planning Education and Research* 34, 1: 45–59.

Cao, Kung and Jean Hillier (2013). "Planning Theory in China and Chinese Planning Theory," *Planning Theory* 12, 4: 331–334.

Chadwick, George (1971). *A Systems View of Planning*. Oxford: Pergamon Press.

Christensen, Karen (1985). "Coping with Uncertainty in Planning," *Journal of the American Planning Association* 51, 1: 63–73.

Clavel, Pierre (1986). *The Progressive City: Planning and Participation, 1969–1984*. New Brunswick, NJ: Rutgers University Press.

Connell, David J. (2010). "Schools of Planning Thought," *International Planning Studies* 15, 4: 335–345.

Corburn, Jason (2005). *Street Science: Community Knowledge and Environmental Health*. Cambridge, MA: The MIT Press.

Corburn, Jason (2003). "Bringing Local Knowledge into Environmental Decision Making," *Journal of Planning Education and Research* 22, 4: 420–433.

Dalton, Linda C. (1989). "Emerging Knowledge about Planning Practice," *Journal of Planning Education and Research* 9, 1: 29–44.

Davidoff, Paul (1965). "Advocacy and Pluralism in Planning," *Journal of the American Institute of Planners* 31, 4: 331–338.

Davidoff, Paul and Thomas A. Reiner (1962). "A Choice Theory of Planning," *Journal of the American Institute of Planners* 28, 2: 103–115.

Davoudi, Simin (2015). "Planning as Practice of Knowing," *Planning Theory* 14, 3: 316–331.

Day, Diane (1997). "Citizen Participation in the Planning Process," *Journal of Planning Literature* 11, 3: 421–434.

Dubrucká, Lucia (2016). "Reframing Planning Theory in Terms of Five Categories of Questions," *Planning Theory* 15, 2: 145–161.

Dyckman, John W. (1983). "Reflections on Planning Practice in an Age of Reaction," *Journal of Planning Education and Research* 3, 3: 5–12.

Dyckman, John W. (1969). "The Practical Uses of Planning Theory," *Journal of the American Institute of Planners* 35, 3: 298–300.

Dyckman, John W. (1961). "Planning and Decision Theory," *Journal of the American Institute of Planners* 27, 4: 335–345.

Etzioni, Amitai (1967). "Mixed Scanning: A 'Third' Approach to Decision-Making," *Public Administration Review* 27, 5: 385–392.

Fainstein, Norman I. and Susan S. Fainstein (1979). "New Debates in Urban Planning: The Impact of Marxist Theory within the United States," *International Journal of Urban and Regional Research* 3, 3: 381–403.

Fainstein, Susan S. (2010). *The Just City*. Ithaca, NY: Cornell University Press.

Fainstein, Susan S. (2008). "Planning and the Just City," *Harvard Design Magazine* no. 27: 70–76.

Fainstein, Susan S. (2005a). "Planning Theory and the City," *Journal of Planning Education and Research* 25, 2: 121–130.

Fainstein, Susan S. (2005b). "The Return of Urban Renewal," *Harvard Design Magazine* no. 22: 1–5.

Fainstein, Susan S. (2000). "New Directions in Planning Theory," *Urban Affairs Review* 35, 4: 451–478.

Fainstein, Susan S. and Scott Campbell (2012). "Introduction: The Structure and Debates of Planning Theory," pp. 1–20 in Susan S. Fainstein and Scott Campbell, eds, *Readings in Planning Theory*. Malden, MA: Wiley-Blackwell.

Faludi, Andreas (1973). *Planning Theory*. Oxford: Pergamon Press.

Flyvbjerg, Bent (2001). *Making Social Science Matter*. Cambridge: Cambridge University Press.

Flyvbjerg, Bent (1998). *Rationality and Power: Democracy in Practice*. Chicago, IL: University of Chicago Press.

Fogelsong, Richard E. (1986). *Planning the Capitalist City*. Princeton, NJ: Princeton University Press.

Forester, John (2011). "Planning's Dirty Little Secrets and Its Implications," *Planning Theory and Practice* 12, 3: 325–328.

Forester, John (2009). *Dealing with Differences: Dramas of Mediating Public Disputes*. New York: Oxford University Press.

Forester, John (1999). "Reflections on the Future Understanding of Planning Practice," *International Planning Studies* 4, 2: 175–193.

Forester, John (1996). "Argument, Power and Passion in Planning," pp. 241–262 in Seymour J. Mandelbaum, Luigi Mazza, and Robert W. Burchell, eds, *Explorations in Planning Theory*. New Brunswick, NJ: CUPR Press.

Forester, John (1989). *Planning in the Face of Power*. Berkeley, CA: University of California Press.

Frick, Karen Trapenberg (2013). "The Actions of Discontent," *Journal of the American Planning Association* 79, 3: 190–200.

Friedman, Joel, Judith Kossy, and Mitt Regan (1980). "Working within the State: The Role of the Progressive Planner," pp. 251–278 in Pierre Clavel, John Forester, and William W. Goldsmith, eds, *Urban and Regional Planning in an Age of Austerity*. New York: Pergamon Press.

Friedmann, John (2005). "Globalization and the Emerging Cultures of Planning," *Progress in Planning* 64, 3: 183–234.

Friedmann, John (1992). *Empowerment: The Politics of Alternative Development*. Cambridge, MA: Blackwell.

Friedmann, John (1989). "Planning in the Public Domain: Discourse and Praxis," *Journal of Planning Education and Research* 8, 2: 128–130.

Friedmann, John (1987). *Planning in the Public Domain*. Princeton, NJ: Princeton University Press.

Friedmann, John and Barclay Hudson (1974). "Knowledge and Action: A Guide to Planning Theory," *Journal of the American Institute of Planners* 40, 4: 2–16.

Glass, Ruth (1959). "The Evaluation of Planning: Some Sociological Considerations," *International Social Science Journal* 11, 3: 393–409.

Gleeson, Brendan and Nicholas Low (2000). "Is Planning History?" pp. 269–284 in Robert Firestone, ed., *Urban Planning in a Changing World*. London: E. & F.N. Spon.

Gualini, Enrico (2015). "Conflict in the City," pp. 3–36 in Enrico Gualini, ed., *Planning and Conflict*. New York: Routledge.

Gunder, Michael (2010a). "Planning as the Ideology of (Neoliberal) Space," *Planning Theory* 9, 4: 298–314.

Gunder, Michael (2010b). "Making Planning Theory Matter: A Lacanian Encounter with *Phronesis*," *International Planning Studies* 15, 1: 37–51.

Hague, C. (1991). "A Review of Planning Theory in Britain," *Town Planning Review* 62, 3: 295–310.

Hall, Peter, ed. (2002). *Cities of Tomorrow*. Malden, MA: Blackwell.

Harper, Thomas L. and Stanley M. Stein (1992). "The Centrality of Narrative Ethical Theory to Contemporary Planning Theory," *Journal of Planning Education and Research* 11, 2: 105–116.

Harris, Britton (1997). "The Theory of Planning and of Its Profession," *Environment and Planning B* 24, 2: 483–492.

Harrison, Philip (2014). "Making Planning Theory Real," *Planning Theory* 12, 1: 65–81.

Harrison, Philip (2006). "On the Edge of Reason," *Urban Studies* 43, 2: 319–335.

Harvey, David (1978). "On Planning the Ideology of Planning," pp. 213–233 in Robert W. Burchell and George Sternlieb, eds, *Planning Theory in the 1980s: A Search for Future Directions*. New Brunswick, NJ: CUPR Press.

Hayek, Friedrich A. (1944). *The Road to Serfdom*. Chicago, IL: University of Chicago Press.

Healey, Patsy (2009). "The Pragmatic Tradition in Planning Thought," *Journal of Planning Education and Research* 28, 3: 277–292.

Healey, Patsy, ed. (2006). *Collaborative Planning*. New York: Palgrave Macmillan.

Healey, Patsy (1992a). "A Planner's Day: Knowledge and Action in Communicative Planning," *Journal of the American Planning Association* 58, 1: 9–20.

Healey, Patsy (1992b). "Planning through Debate," *Town Planning Review* 63, 2: 143–162.

Hendler, Sue (1996). "On the Use of Models in Planning Theory," pp. 400–413 in Seymour J. Mandelbaum, Luigi Mazza, and Robert W. Burchell, eds, *Explorations in Planning Theory*. New Brunswick, NJ: CUPR Press.

Hendler, Sue (1994). "Feminist Planning Ethics," *Journal of Planning Literature* 9, 2: 115–127.

Hendler, Sue (1991). "Ethics in Planning," *Journal of Planning Education and Research* 10, 2: 99–105.

Hillier, Jean (1995). "The Unwritten Law of Planning Theory: Common Sense," *Journal of Planning Education and Research* 14, 4: 292–296.

Hoch, Charles (1992). "The Paradox of Power in Planning Practice," *Journal of Planning Education and Research* 11, 3: 206–215.

Hoch, Charles (1984a). "Doing Good and Being Right," *Journal of the American Planning Association* 50, 3: 335–345.

Hoch, Charles (1984b). "Pragmatism, Planning, and Power," *Journal of Planning Education and Research* 4, 2: 86–95.

Hoover, Robert C. (1961). "A View of Ethics and Planning," *Journal of the American Institute of Planners* 27, 4: 293–304.

Howe, Elizabeth (1979). "The Ethics of Contemporary American Planners," *Journal of the American Planning Association* 45, 3: 243–255.

Huxley, Margo (2000). "The Limits to Communicative Planning," *Journal of Planning Education and Research* 19, 4: 369–377.

Huxley, Margo and Oren Yiftachel (2000). "New Paradigms or Old Myopias? Unsettling the Communicative Turn in Planning Theory," *Journal of Planning Education and Research* 19, 4: 333–342.

Innes, Judith E. (1995). "Planning Theory's Emerging Paradigm," *Journal of Planning Education and Research* 14, 3: 183–189.

Innes, Judith E. and David E. Booher (2010). *Planning with Complexity*. New York: Routledge.

Innes, Judith E. and David E. Booher (2004). "Reframing Public Participation," *Planning Theory and Practice* 5, 4: 419–436.

Innes, Judith E. and David E. Booher (1999). "Consensus Building as Role Playing and Bricolage," *Journal of the American Planning Association* 65, 1: 9–26.

Klosterman, Richard E. (1980). "A Public Interest Criterion," *Journal of the American Planning Association* 46, 3: 323–333.

Knieling, Joerg and Frank Othengraften, eds (2009). *Planning Cultures in Europe*. Farnham: Ashgate.

Krumholz, Norman (1982). "A Retrospective View of Equity Planning," *Journal of the American Planning Association* 48, 2: 163–174.

Lai, L.W.C. (1999). "Hayek and Town Planning," *Environment and Planning A* 31, 9: 1567–1582.

Lake, Robert W. (2016). "Justice as Subject and Object of Planning," *International Journal of Urban and Regional Research* 40, 6: 1205–1220.

Lake, Robert W. and Andrew W. Zitcer (2012). "Who Says? Authority, Voice and Authorship in Narratives of Planning Research," *Journal of Planning Education and Research* 32, 4: 389–399.

Laurien, Lucie, Maxine Day, Michael Backhurst, et al. (2004). "What Drives Planning Implementation?: Plans, Planning Agencies and Developers," *Journal of Environmental Planning and Management* 47, 4: 555–577.

Leino, Helena, Ilari Karppi, and Ari Jokinen (2017). "It's All about the Birds! Non-Human Actors' Situational Power in Creating Conditions for Human Engagement," *Planning Theory* 16, 2: 133–149.

Levy, Sara, Kariel Martens, and Ros van der Heijden (2016). "Agent-Based Models and Self-Organization," *Town Planning Review* 87, 3: 321–338.

Lichfield, Nathaniel (1968). "Economics in Town Planning: A Basis for Decision Making," *Town Planning Review* 39, 1: 5–20.

Lieto, Laura and Robert A. Beauregard (2013). "Planning for a Material World," *Crios* 6: 11–20.

Lim, Gill-Chin (1986). "Toward a Synthesis of Contemporary Planning Theories," *Journal of Planning Education and Research* 5, 2: 75–85.

Lindblom, Charles (1959). "The Science of 'Muddling Through'," *Public Administration Review* 19, 2: 79–88.

Lopes de Souza, Marcelo (2006). "Social Movements as Critical Urban Planning," *City* 10, 3: 327–342.

Lord, Alex (2013). "Towards a Non-Theoretical Understanding of Planning," *Planning Theory* 13, 1: 26–43.

Lovering, John (2009). "The Recession and the End of Planning as We Know It," *International Planning Studies* 14, 1: 1–6.

Low, Nicholas (1991). *Planning, Politics and the State*. London: Unwin Hyman.

Mabin, Alan and Dan Smit (1997). "Reconsidering South Africa's Cities? The Making of Urban Planning 1900–2000," *Planning Perspectives* 12, 2: 193–223.

March, Alan (2010). "Practising Theory: When Theory Affects Urban Planning," *Planning Theory* 9, 2: 108–125.

Marcuse, Peter (2009). "From Critical Urban Theory to the Right to the City," *City* 13, 2–3: 185–197.

Marcuse, Peter (1976). "Professional Ethics and Beyond," *Journal of the American Planning Association* 42, 3: 264–274.

Marris, Peter (1975, orig. 1974). *Loss and Change*. New York: Anchor Press.

Mazza, Luigio (1995). "Technical Knowledge, Practical Reason and the Planner's Responsibility," *Town Planning Review* 66, 4: 389–409.

Mazza, Luigi and Marco Bianconi (2014). "Which Aims and Knowledge for Spatial Planning?" *Town Planning Review* 85, 4: 513–531.

Meth, Paula (2010). "Unsettling Insurgency," *Planning Theory and Practice* 11, 2: 241–262.

Metzger, Jonathan, Linda Soneryd, and Kristina Tamm Hallström (2017). "'Power' Is That Which Remains to Be Explained," *Planning Theory* 16, 2: 203–222.

Meyerson, Martin (1956). "Beyond the Middle-Range Bridge for Comprehensive Planning," *Journal of the American Institute of Planners* 22, 2: 58–64.

Meyerson, Martin and Edward Banfield (1955). *Politics, Planning and the Public Interest*. Glencoe, IL: The Free Press.

Miraftab, Faranak (2009). "Insurgent Planning: Situating Radical Planning in the Global South," *Planning Theory* 8, 1: 32–50.

Monno, Valeria and Abdul Khakee (2012). "Tokenism or Political Activism?" *International Planning Studies* 17, 1: 85–101.

Moroni, Stefano (2010a). "An Evolutionary Theory of Institutions and a Dynamic Approach to Reform," *Planning Theory* 9, 4: 275–297.

Moroni, Stefano (2010b). "Rethinking the Theory and Practice of Land-Use Regulation," *Planning Theory* 9, 2: 137–155.

Moroni, Stefano (2004). "Towards a Reconstruction of the Public Interest Criterion," *Planning Theory* 3, 2: 151–171.

Musser, Ian (1980). "The Limits to Planning," *Town Planning Review* 51, 1: 39–49.

Needleman, Martin and Carolyn Needleman (1974). *Guerillas in the Bureaucracy*. New York: John Wiley & Sons.

Osborne, Natalie and Deanna Grant-Smith (2015). "Supporting Mindful Planners in a Mindless System," *Town Planning Review* 86, 6: 677–698.

Perloff, Harvey (1957). *Education for Planning: City, State, and Region*. Baltimore, MD: Johns Hopkins University Press.

Pløger, John (2004). "Strife: Urban Planning and Agonism," *Planning Theory* 7, 1: 71–92.

Pressman, Jeffrey and Aaron Wildavsky (1973). *Implementation*. Berkeley, CA: University of California Press.

Rabinovitz, Francine (1969). *City Politics and Planning*. New Brunswick, NJ: Transaction Publishers.

Rauws, Ward (2016). "Civic Initiatives in Urban Development," *Town Planning Review* 87, 3: 339–361.

Reynolds, Josephine P. (1969). "Public Participation in Planning," *Town Planning Review* 40, 2: 131–148.

Rittel, Horst W.J. and Melvin Webber (1973). "Dilemmas in a General Theory of Planning," *Policy Sciences* 4, 2: 155–169.

Roweis, Shoukry T. (1981). "Urban Planning in Early and Late Capitalist Societies," pp. 159–177 in Michael Dear and Allen Scott, eds, *Urbanization and Urban Planning in Capitalist Society*. London: Methuen.

Roy, Ananya (2011). "Commentary: Placing Planning in the World – Transnationalism as Practice and Critique," *Journal of Planning Education and Research* 31, 4: 406–415.

Roy, Ananya (2008). "Post-Liberalism: On the Ethico-Politics of Planning," *Planning Theory* 7, 1: 92–102.

Rydin, Yvonne (2014). "Comment: The Challenges of the 'Material Turn' for Planning Studies," *Planning Theory and Practice* 15, 4: 590–595.

Rydin, Yvonne (2012). "Using Actor-Network Theory to Understand Planning Practice," *Planning Theory* 12, 1: 23–45.

Rydin, Yvonne and Laura Tate, eds (2016). *Actor Networks of Planning*. London: Routledge.

Saarkoski, Heli (2002). "Naturalized Epistemology and Dilemmas of Planning Practice," *Journal of Planning Education and Research* 22, 1: 3–14.

Sager, Tore (2013). *Revising Critical Planning Theory*. London: Routledge.

Sanchez, Thomas W. and Nader Afzalan (2018). "Mapping the Knowledge Domain of Urban Planning," pp. 69–84 in Thomas W. Sanchez, ed., *Planning Knowledge and Research*. New York: Routledge.

Sandercock, Leonie (2003). "Out of the Closet: The Importance of Stories and Storytelling in Planning Practice," *Planning Theory and Practice* 4, 1: 11–28.

Sandercock, Leonie (1998). *Towards Cosmopolis*. Chichester: John Wiley & Sons.

Sandercock, Leonie (1995). "Voices from the Borderlands," *Journal of Planning Education and Research* 14, 2: 77–88.

Sandercock, Leonie and Ann Forsyth (1992). "A Gender Agenda," *Journal of the American Planning Association* 58, 1: 49–59.

Sanyal, Bish (2002). "Globalization, Ethical Compromise and Planning Theory," *Planning Theory* 1, 2: 116–123.

Sarbib, Jean-Lois (1983). "The University of Chicago Program in Planning: A Retrospective Look," *Journal of Planning Education and Research* 2, 2: 77–81.

Schön, Donald (1983). *The Reflective Practitioner: How Professionals Think in Action*. New York: Basic Books.

Schön, Donald (1982). "Some of What a Planner Knows," *Journal of the American Planning Association* 48, 3: 351–364.

Schweitzer, Lisa (2016). "Restorative Planning Ethics: The Therapeutic Imagination and Planning in Public Institutions," *Planning Theory* 15, 2: 130–144.

Shmueli, Deborah F., Sandra Kaufman, and Connie Ozawa (2008). "Mining Negotiation Theory for Planning Insights," *Journal of Planning Education and Research* 27, 3: 359–364.

Shrestha, Pranito and Rulee Aranyu (2015). "Claiming Invited and Invented Spaces: Contingencies for Insurgent Planning Practices," *International Planning Studies* 20, 4: 424–443.

Sorensen, Tony and Martin Auster (1999). "Theory and Practice in Planning," *Australian Planner* 36, 3: 146–149.

Spain, Daphne (2001). *How Women Saved the City*. Minneapolis, MN: University of Minnesota Press.

Tait, Malcolm (2016). "Planning and the Public Interest," *Planning Theory* 15, 4: 335–343.

Talen, Emily (1997). "Success, Failure, and Conformance: An Alternative Approach to Plan Evaluation," *Environment and Planning B* 24, 2: 573–587.

Talen, Emily (1996). "Do Plans Get Implemented?" *Journal of Planning Literature* 10, 3: 248–259.

Taşan-Kok, Tuna (2012). "Contradictions of Neoliberal Urban Planning," pp. 1–19 in Tuna Taşan-Kok and Guy Baeten, eds, *Contradictions of Neoliberal Planning*. Dordrecht: Springer.

Taylor, Nigel (1998). *Urban Planning Theory since 1945*. London: Sage.

Thorpe, Amelia (2017). "Rethinking Participation, Rethinking Planning," *Planning Theory and Practice* 18, 4: 566–582.

Throgmorton, James (2000). "On the Virtues of Skillful Meandering," *Journal of the American Planning Association* 66, 4: 367–379.

Throgmorton, James (1996). "'Impeaching' Research: Planning as Persuasive and Constitutive Discourse," pp. 345–364 in Seymour J. Mandelbaum, Luigi Mazza, and Robert W. Burchell, eds, *Explorations in Planning Theory*. New Brunswick, NJ: CUPR Press.

Uitermark, Justus and Walter Nicholls (2017). "Planning for Social Justice," *Planning Theory* 16, 1: 32–50.

Umemoto, Karen (2001). "Walking in Another's Shoe: Epistemological Challenges in Participatory Planning," *Journal of Planning Education and Research* 21, 1: 17–31.

Van der Goot, A. and T.S. Simey (1949). "The Sociological Approach to Planning," *Town Planning Review* 20, 2: 162–168.

Ward, Stephen (2002). *Planning in the Twentieth-Century City*. Chichester: John Wiley & Sons.

Watson, Vanessa (2008). "Down to Earth: Linking Planning Theory and Practice in the 'Metropole' and Beyond," *International Planning Studies* 13, 3: 223–237.

Watson, Vanessa (2006). "Deep Difference: Diversity, Planning and Ethics," *Planning Theory* 5, 1: 31–50.

Watson, Vanessa (2003). "Conflicting Rationalities: Implications for Planning Theory and Ethics," *Planning Theory and Practice* 4, 4: 395–407.

Webb, David (2018). "Tactical Urbanism," *Planning Theory and Practice* 19, 1: 58–73.

Whittemore, Andrew H. (2014). "Phenomenology and City Planning," *Journal of Planning Education and Research* 34, 3: 301–308.

Wildavsky, Aaron (1973). "If Planning Is Everything, Maybe It's Nothing," *Policy Sciences* 4, 2: 127–153.

Winkler, Tanya (2011). "Retracking Johannesburg: Spaces for Participation and Policymaking," *Journal of Planning Education and Research* 31, 3: 258–271.

Yiftachel, Oren (2006). "Re-Engaging Planning Theory? Towards 'South-Eastern' Perspectives," *Planning Theory* 5, 3: 211–222.

Yiftachel, Oren (1998). "Planning and Social Control," *Journal of Planning Literature* 12, 4: 395–406.

Yiftachel, Oren (1996). "The Internal Frontier: Territorial Control and Ethnic Relations in Israel," *Regional Studies* 30, 5: 493–508.

Yiftachel, Oren (1989). "Towards a New Typology of Urban Planning Theories," *Environment and Planning B* 16, 1: 23–29.

Young, Iris Marion (2011). *Responsibility for Justice*. New York: Oxford University Press.

Index

Titles in the **Elgar Advanced Introductions** series include: